USBORNE

SOCIAL
MEDIA
SURVIVAL GUIDE

Expert advice from

Lindsay Buck
Senior Education Projects Officer
Childnet International
◯ Childnet

Danni Gordon
The Chachi Power Project

USBORNE

SOCIAL MEDIA SURVIVAL GUIDE

Holly Bathie

Designed by
Stephanie Jeffries

Illustrated by

**Richard Merritt, Kate Sutton
and The Boy Fitz Hammond**

Edited by
Felicity Brooks

▶▶▶ Usborne Quicklinks

The internet is a great source of information, but it's very important to know which sites you can trust.

We have selected some useful websites to supplement the information in this book and these are available at **Usborne Quicklinks.** Here you can find more advice around body image, bullying, mental health, and inappropriate images, as well as where to go for help.

For links to all these sites, go to:
usborne.com/Quicklinks
and type in the title of this book
or scan the QR code below.

Please follow the internet safety guidelines at Usborne Quicklinks. Children should be supervised online.

Introduction

Whether you use social media or not, it can be difficult to ignore this global online world. Sometimes you, or people you know, might spend more time on social media than doing anything else!

This book will answer questions about all different aspects of social media, **the good** <u>and</u> **the bad,** as well as how to get a bit of time and space away from it when you need to. It may also be able to help you with any topics you're not comfortable searching for online, or asking your friends or family about.

Whenever you see a word or phrase in a box, (**like this**), you will find more information about it in the glossary which starts on page 283.

Contents

Chapter 1

What is social media? The basics

Let's start at the beginning – social media websites and (apps) allow you to **socialize online,** wherever you are.

// OFF TO THE FOOTBALL MATCH. WISH US LUCK GUYS!! //

They make it easy to chat, message and share photos and videos with others. Even gaming sites are a type of social media, where you can talk with friends and meet new people.

These apps are designed for people to connect with each other and feel like part of a community. These connections create a [**network**]. It's a bit like meeting someone new at a party and finding out how you both know the host.

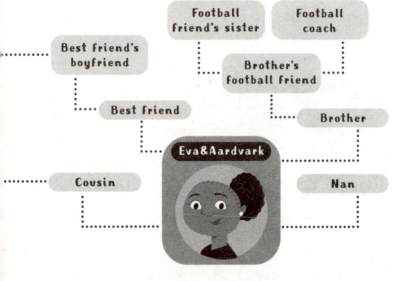

Depending on the app, your contacts and the people who connect with you could be called friends, [**followers**] or [**subscribers**].

How does it work?

Social media users set up an account, with a username, a picture and a profile page.

See **Chapter 2** for how to do this safely.

Users then post [**content**] on their [**profile**], such as their own thoughts and feelings, photos, videos or [**links**].

Once you have read someone's post, you could choose to [**like**] or comment on it.

If it's something interesting, important or funny, you might decide to [**share**] it, which means you can forward it on to others.

Number of shares

⊘ 54 ⊙ 13   Shared by **TheRightJackson**

Gorillas eat ALL DAY LONG. Wish I could eat cake all day long...

⊘ ● ⊙   Click to **SHARE**

Comments:
5 mins ago **LetsBNisha**
Haha, this is so me!

You could also click on someone's profile to see more about what they are up to, or to send them a private (also known as 'direct') message.

⊘ 54 ⊙ 13   Shared by **TheRightJackson**

Gorillas eat ALL DAY LONG. Wish I could eat cake all day long...

⊘ ● ⊙

Click the name to send a direct message or see their **PROFILE**

TheRightJackson

Often the main page you see when you log in to an app is your [feed], which shows what your contacts have recently posted and commented on.

5 mins ago Sageguy15

I *LOVE* Hot Shots Café. The beans are excellent.
#HotShotsCafé

3 mins ago Lulu&I
Ohhh yes, I'm hungry now!!!

5 mins ago Petey_Man338
My favourite are the tacos @Sageguy15. Yummy

⊘12 ▶4   5 mins ago Jenni_Blout

Chill OUT   Can't wait for the weekend. Roll on Friday!!!

⊘ 💬 ▶

10 mins ago QweenNSprinkles

Check out Nikhil's moves on the slopes :-) I was not so good...
#BoardSchool

⊘6 ▶2   Shared by WrightRonWrites

Can anyone recommend a good BARBER near me?

13

@Simrah_The344

@Ondon_Donny

Tagging

To draw a particular friend's attention to something, you could 'tag' them by typing their username in your post (on some apps you need to use an **@** 'at' symbol first). Your friend will then receive a (**notification**) from the app. Most apps also notify you each time one of your posts has been commented on, liked or shared.

@tag_your_friends

The **@** tag will become a direct link to your friend's profile, so tagging someone also draws attention to them. (Do think about whether your friend would be happy to be tagged in your post.)

#hashtagging

Some social media apps encourage tagging words, using a **#** 'hash' symbol to draw attention to certain topics.

You can learn more about this in **Chapter 15**.

Public and private

All apps offer slightly different things, but there are **two main types** – some are public-facing, and some are more private.

Public-facing apps are designed to be online spaces where strangers can inspire each other and share news and ideas. More private ones are focused on daily conversations and updates between friends.

Whichever type of app you use, social media allows you to **connect** and keep up to date with <u>many more people than you would be able to in person</u>. There are advantages to using social media to connect with lots of people.

You could:

- Make friends with people anywhere, even on the other side of the world.

- Learn all sorts of new skills through homemade 'how-to' videos.

- Find others who share an interest or passion of yours, and form or join an online club.

- Reach a wider audience if you are fundraising, or if you want to raise awareness of a local or national cause that you care about.

- See thoughts, photos and videos posted by famous people.

- Share photos and videos of things you have done or made, and get lots of useful or positive feedback on them.

- Watch photos and videos of all sorts of funny and clever things people have made or done, that you would never have thought of.

Are there any disadvantages?

Whichever apps you use, you can have lots of conversations going on at once. It can feel like EVERYONE is on social media, including all your friends.

Although it's a lot of fun chatting and laughing with your friends in this way, **there are downsides** to having your conversations recorded online.

It's easy to forget what someone has said face-to-face or over the phone, <u>but anything you post online gets backed up somewhere</u>. People could also download your photos and videos, or take screenshots of your posts.

That means if you post or share something you later regret, even if it gets deleted, there may always be a record of it.

You can learn more about this in **Chapter 3**.

Other not-so-fun aspects of social media could include:

- ☹ Unwanted attention from strangers.
- ☹ Receiving criticism and negative opinions on your posts.
- ☹ Online bullying.
- ☹ Seeing things you wish you hadn't.
- ☹ Difficulty avoiding bad language and offensive content.
- ☹ Endless advertising.
- ☹ Constant comparison with others (which can affect your mental health).
- ☹ Seeing less of your friends and family in person.

Is it for me?

With so many different social media apps and ways to use them – plus different attitudes of your friends and parents towards what you should and shouldn't be doing on social media – it can feel **overwhelming**.

Social media is a part of everyday life for many people, so even if you don't intend to use it much (or at all), it's good to know how to use it **safely,** so that you and your friends don't get caught out in the future.

Chapter 2

Setting up and using your account safely

If you decide you want to join social media (and you certainly don't have to), think about what you would like to use it for. There are **LOTS** of different apps to choose from. You could use only one app, or a few. Some apps focus on sharing videos, some on sharing photos, and some are great for just chatting or playing online.

Social media apps are free to download, but you must be **OVER 13** to be able to create a social media account, and often you need parental permission to create an account if you are **UNDER 18.** If you want to join social media, talk to your parents or carers about the apps you would like to use.

Signing up

Often you sign up with your email address and a password. Make sure your password is a **strong** one, including numbers, both capital and lowercase letters, and at least one symbol. It should be something you can remember, but not obvious.

A strong password is essential because some (hackers) spend their time trying to work out people's passwords to take over their accounts.

On most apps, you can choose to stay signed in, so the app remembers your password. This is handy, **BUT not as safe as logging in** <u>each time</u> **you open the app.** You don't want someone sneaking onto your phone and posting something on your social media pretending to be YOU.

Hee! Hee! I'm going to embarrass my sister!

Introducing yourself

Next you need a username, which is the name that will appear to other people on the app. It's best to <u>avoid using your own name</u>. On most apps, your username can be **ANYTHING** you choose.

On most apps, you can then create your own profile, which is an area that's all about **YOU**. You can choose what to put on there, such as a photo or an (avatar) (illustration) and a (bio) (short for biography) about your interests.

Eva&Aardvark

I'm Eva. I love ALL sports, especially hockey and cricket.

My favourite food of all time is spaghetti and meatballs!! Yum :)

Some apps have a form with lots of questions you could fill in to make your profile more detailed, such as your age, gender, or where you live. <u>DON'T put any of that personal information on your profile.</u> Your friends already know it, and it's none of a stranger's business.

Privacy please!

Whichever app you use, your account
will be public by default (automatically).
This means that your profile and posts
can be seen by ANYONE using the app,
including strangers, unless you **look
carefully at your privacy settings.**

Apps have different privacy settings
and features, so for each app you use
it's worth finding the 'settings' part of
your account and having a browse.

You may be able to:

- Choose 'friends only', in your privacy settings, so that anything you post is only seen by the people you have chosen to connect with on the app — your contacts.

- Select so that only your friends and contacts are allowed to send you a private (or direct) message.

  See **Chapter 13** for more about direct messages.

- Limit how much of your profile people see if they are not one of your contacts.

If in doubt, <u>choose the highest possible privacy settings</u>. All of this is designed to protect you from unwanted contact by strangers, and puts you in control when you are using social media.

Don't give yourself away

Even if you use the highest privacy settings, there are some things you should <u>NEVER</u> post, such as:

- **X** your phone number
- **X** your home address
- **X** your bank account details
- **X** where you hide the spare key to your house!

EVERYONE is a
stranger until they
get to know you.

Always **STOP** and **THINK** before accepting
any connection request on social media.
Adding someone as a friend or contact
means they can comment on all your
photos and see what you are up to.

Be as choosy about who you are friends
with online as you are in person. Don't
worry about seeming rude by turning
down a request from someone you haven't
met in person. It's hard enough making
time for your real friends!

Where did you say you were going?

Even if you don't intentionally connect with strangers on social media, it's **important** that you <u>DON'T</u> post information that <u>might allow a stranger to find you offline.</u>

Don't talk about, or post pictures of, your house or school, and don't tag your location when you're out and about. In 'settings' you can double-check that the app doesn't automatically tag your location.

I'm in the park on Knight's Way.

Think about your friends' safety and privacy, too. Don't location tag them, or post photos or videos of them without their permission.

STAY SAFE

Some apps have map features that are designed for people to tag their location to see where the nearest coffee shop is, and who else is nearby to meet up. It sounds fun, and it's nice to have online 'followers', <u>but you don't want to be actually followed anywhere.</u> So it's a good idea **NOT** to use these features.

TheRightJackson

Just realized I've got 273 friends on social media! Haha. Popular.

Eva&Aardvark

Ha. I removed loads of mine. Too many photos of people's dinner...

TheRightJackson

Yeah true, half these people I don't really know.

Eva&Aardvark

You should totally go through and remove some. A spring clean!

TheRightJackson

Mmmm, I'd feel bad... what if they notice?

Eva&Aardvark

You don't want loads of strangers seeing all your updates though.

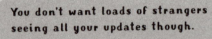

Chapter 3

Your persona and online reputation

Who you are online

Every time you post on social media, you add to the perception others have of you. This is your **persona,** which is the personality you present to others online. Because it's something you create, it's tempting to make it a 'better' version of your real self and bend the truth a bit.

Is this a true reflection of me?

If your posts are all about you, though – endless (**selfies**), for example – you could come across as self-centred. If you share and talk about things other than **you, you, you** all the time, you might get more positive reactions to your posts than if you try too hard to show off.

Just the highlights

Your social media profile is an <u>edited version</u> of your life. It's understandable to want to show only the flattering photos, fun trips and proud moments.

But just as **YOU** can be selective about what you post, so can other people. Not everyone is as **happy, popular** or **successful** as they seem on social media. Photos in particular don't tell the whole truth.

You are not the only one who might feel sad, bad, ugly or a bit of a failure at times. People might look at **YOUR** profile and think your life is perfect and nothing ever goes wrong for you, which is probably not the case!

ONLINE

// MY LIFE IS SO GREAT! //

// I FEEL SO ALONE... //

OFFLINE

Fake personas

If someone posts lots of videos of cats doing funny things, you'd assume they like cats and have a sense of humour. Their persona is that of a cheerful 'cat person'.

Ugh. I HATE cats.

We humans are quite lazy about making assumptions, which makes it straightforward for anyone to create a particular online persona. But that persona might be **completely different** to how that person is in real life.

There's a saying: "On the internet, no one knows you're a dog". Although there aren't really any canines posting online, <u>ANYONE can pretend to be someone else on social media.</u>

36

You might like to come across as a completely different person on social media. Perhaps you want to create a certain 'public image', or a wacky alter-ego. But always remember, if you are making up a social media identity, other people might be too.

See **Chapters 13 and 14** for more about keeping yourself safe from adults who are not who they say they are.

Protecting your reputation

Your online identity is not just a collection of posts, photos and videos. The way you act on social media, and the things other people post about you, also add to it. Your online identity builds up a **reputation,** and what you do online leaves a (digital footprint). Digital footprints are difficult to erase, so mistakes can follow you.

Oversharing

Social media can feel like a private place to confess things, <u>but it really isn't</u>. Although you can adjust your privacy settings so that your posts can only be seen by your contacts, you can't control what they then share. That means **anything you post** could be shared beyond your friendship group, right across social media.

I'll only send this to a couple of friends...

WOW! This is too good not to share!

Ha ha! Shared.

Be careful about posting photos and videos that could embarrass you, or someone else, if they were shared more widely.

No way!

'Do I really want to post this?' checklist

☐ Would you mind if your nan/worst enemy/ future love of your life saw this?

☐ If you're talking about someone, is this something you wouldn't say to their face?

☐ If you were applying for a job, or course, would you be embarrassed if the interviewers saw this?

☐ Are you going to end up worrying about what you've posted afterwards?

If you ticked **ANY** of these, it's <u>NOT</u> worth posting.

What, that old thing?

You might not think your post is a problem now, but it's worth considering if it will cause problems for you in the future. Old posts are not automatically deleted. That means **whatever you put online will stay there,** waiting to be dug up by your future blind date, future job interviewer, maybe even your grandchildren.

Still perfectly preserved, 300 years later!

If you search for your own name online, you might be surprised about what appears. Social media posts can also turn up in certain online searches, so teachers, parents and other adults may stumble upon something you REALLY DON'T want them to see.

5 YEARS AGO...

The online reputation you build up now could be difficult to shrug off when you are older. Some companies, schools, charities and other employers do **social media background checks** on interview candidates. You may not get hired because of something you posted on social media, <u>however long ago it was</u>. If it's down to you and one other person for the job, the company might make the final decision based on your online persona.

Be considerate

Think of other people's reputations too. If you write something rude or untrue about someone, or post an embarrassing photo or video of them, you're taking away their ability to be in charge of their online reputation, which isn't fair.

Why did she post that?

#that's_not_me_anymore

If there is something <u>seriously inaccurate</u> about you online, it may be possible to get it removed from searches (although not from the internet).

There's information about asking search engines to take down links about you at **Usborne Quicklinks**. (See page 4 for more.)

Cleaning up your reputation

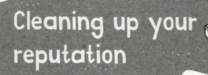

If you've stopped using a social media app, or other site, then **deactivate your profile** (in 'settings'). If old posts don't represent who you are now, then remove them if you can. That also goes for sites and apps where you don't post under your real name – someone may still be able to make the link between that account and you.

Mr Shaw, were you once known as 'The Shadow'?

Is it REALLY gone?

Most apps allow you to delete a post, but unfortunately that <u>doesn't</u> mean it's completely disappeared.

Other people may have shared it, or posted screenshots. Social media companies also regularly back up their (**data**), including deleted items.

So... it's always better to be **safe** than **sorry** –

THINK BEFORE YOU POST.

KTsKite

Argh!! Sia has tagged me in the STUPIDEST photo from last year.

WrightRonWrites

Oh no, from her birthday party? Get her to take it down asap!

KTsKite

Messaged her. Really don't need people at my new school seeing that online!

WrightRonWrites

It'll be ok :-)

KTsKite

I hope so. My boss at the café won't be thrilled with it either.

WrightRonWrites

Maybe ask the others from her party not to post pix of you too?

46

Managing your social media

Posting your thoughts and feelings

An advantage of social media is that when you experience something, happy or sad, **you can let ALL your friends know about it at once.** Your social media can act like a noticeboard all about you, so your friends know what is going on in your life when they're not with you in person.

 I won a writing competition!

Mason should definitely *NOT* have been voted off.

 Anyone else nervous about the match tomorrow?

Before you post, though, think about what response, if any, you are after. Is this post a general statement, or do you want to start a conversation or debate?

Eva&Aardvark . 25 mins ago

Well THAT could have gone better...

If you post that you are having a bad day, you might feel great if people comment with positive wishes and (emojis) to cheer you up.

MinotaurQue5ta . 12 mins ago

I was thinking the EXACT same!

Equally, if you post about something you love, you might feel upset if people comment saying something negative. On some social media apps, you can **disable comments** for certain posts, which could be very useful.

Have you thought about...?

If you have lots of thoughts and opinions on a certain subject, you could consider writing your own blog*, rather than writing long posts on social media. You could post a link to your blog, so your friends and contacts know about it. Friends and strangers would still be able to comment with their own thoughts, praise or criticism, unless you disable comments for your whole blog.

FILM BLOG IDEAS
- good and bad
- costume design
- special effects

 BAD FILMS
- Dark Spiders
- Your Lifeline
- Sky Swing
- These Surprises

GOOD FILMS
- Hero Time
- Thunder Gods
- Lizard Life
- Forever You

*Find out more about this at **Usborne Quicklinks,** see page 4.

It can be annoying when a friend's post is intriguing, dramatic, or cryptic... but when you comment asking them about it, they don't reply. It's better not to post something publicly that you know will prompt lots of questions, if actually you don't want to talk about it.

See **Chapter 17** for better ways to get help.

 # Looking for validation

Validation means 'acceptance and approval'. It's natural to want to be liked and included by your friends, and to care about what other people think of you. Social media networks are so large, though, that you could end up looking for validation from an ex-boyfriend's sister's friend's cousin who you'd **never even heard of** until ten minutes ago!

Why hasn't Chris liked my post yet?

Having many likes, shares and social media contacts can really **boost** your self-confidence, but finding you only have a few of these can really **knock** your self-confidence. It's exhausting!

There are so many different ways to look for validation on social media that **you might not even realize you are doing it.** If social media is ever making you feel rubbish about yourself, it's a sign you need to give yourself a break. Don't put your happiness in the hands of people you don't know, and who don't know you beyond your online persona. Turn your attention to other things that make you feel **confident,** that don't depend on the opinions of other people.

I am **REALLY GOOD** at this!

Your friends

Whether you joined social media mainly as way to keep in touch with your current friends, or to make new online friends, the people you choose to connect with on social media will have an impact on how you feel day-to-day.

Perhaps you might strengthen a friendship with someone you've just met in person, or you don't know very well, through sending each other videos of animals doing funny things.

Or you might relax chatting with your online-only friends while you play a game together after a tough day at school.

There are lots of ways social media can make you feel good through connecting with others. Of course, just as you can fall out with your friends in person, you can also have trouble with your friendships on social media. A comment might be taken the wrong way, tagging someone in that (**meme**) might accidentally cause offence, or you might totally disagree with a friend's post.

If you find yourself in an online argument or post something you regret, apologize and, if you can, talk about it with your friend in person. It's always easier to sort something out face-to-face.

I'm worried it all went too far...

If you are worried about a friend's post, or about anything they are saying online, you can find suggestions for how you can help them at **Usborne Quicklinks** (see page 4).

A quick phone call or an in-person chat could easily clear up any mix-ups and misunderstandings.

CALLING ALEX...

How are you doing?

Being on social media can help you feel **connected to others,** and give you a sense of belonging. It can also make you feel in competition with other people who have fabulous-looking online personas. Making constant comparisons will always lead to someone feeling inferior, which isn't a nice feeling at all.

Luckily, there are lots of places to get help, if social media is actually making you feel disconnected. **You are not alone** – whatever you are experiencing, others have experienced that too **AND** found help for it.

See **Chapter 17** for more information about where to get help.

Social media schedule

When everyone's talking on social media, you might feel like you always have to be scrolling through the app so that you don't miss out on something funny or interesting.

If you're on more than one app, there might not be enough hours in the day to keep up!

I wish I could sleep with my eyes open.

Remember to look after YOURSELF, as well as your phone.

Put it on silent or, even better, don't keep it in your room at night so you can get some sleep. You don't have to respond **INSTANTLY** on social media. Think of it like arriving at a party fashionably late. You're a busy person with people to see and homework to do, so <u>that social media debate can wait</u>.

Keeping it real

Maintaining your social media shouldn't become a chore, or a full-time job. If you find yourself **obsessively** checking your phone or thinking about your next post, you may be a bit ADDICTED to social media. The more time you spend online, the less time you spend interacting with people face-to-face, or doing fun activities that are good for your brain and body.

It's important not to neglect your family (they love you!) or your other real-life relationships. A social media like can never replace a real-life hug. (It can't replace your schoolwork, either.)

When you spend so much time posting about what you are doing, you might forget to appreciate your time **OFFLINE**. Sometimes it's better to put away your phone and, **instead of capturing the moment, just enjoy it.**

Axel's online!

PING!

PING!

PING!

16 COMMENTS

New post!

7 LIKES

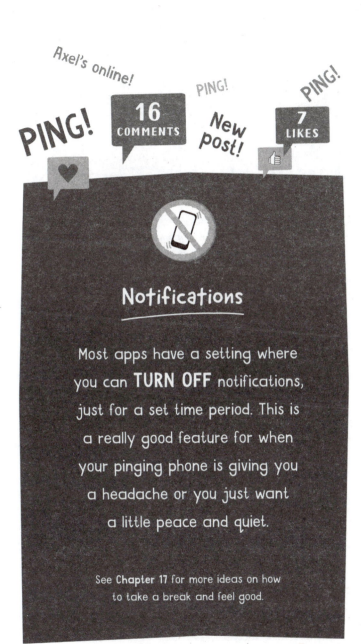

Notifications

Most apps have a setting where you can **TURN OFF** notifications, just for a set time period. This is a really good feature for when your pinging phone is giving you a headache or you just want a little peace and quiet.

See **Chapter 17** for more ideas on how to take a break and feel good.

Eva&Aardvark

So 35 mins after I posted and not a single person has commented :-(

MissT.Surfer

Maybe they just don't know what to say? It is complicated. xx

Eva&Aardvark

I feel so rubbish and just want to know people agree with me.

MissT.Surfer

Oh Eva, you need to get AWAY from social. Get some fresh air? x

Eva&Aardvark

Yeah, you're right.

MissT.Surfer

Why don't I come over later, we can catch up? Love you loads. xxx

Chapter 5

How to avoid trouble

Knowing that you might never actually meet the people you talk to online could make you take **more risks** with what you say, and when you post something public on your social media it's easy to forget just how many people might see it.

Just as in everyday life, there are **consequences** to your actions online too. If you don't keep that in mind, you might find yourself in trouble on social media – from getting into arguments to breaking the law.

Does anyone know?

Public-facing social media apps are great for bringing together people who share an interest in something, such as a book, a game, or a sport, to talk about it in a (**forum**). If someone wants to talk about a particular topic, or ask a question, they can start a discussion and get lots of replies. This is called a (**discussion thread**).

How not to be annoying
on a discussion thread

DON'T SPAM

...that is, don't comment with the same thing over and over again, or post something irrelevant to the discussion. If you want to change the subject, start a new discussion thread and post a link to it instead. That way, your conversations can stay on track.

SHH, SPOILERS

A spoiler is when someone gives away something from a story, film or TV show, that others would rather have had as a surprise. If you want to discuss what happens in a chapter or episode, start your post with:

// SPOILER ALERT //

so people who don't want to know what happens can look away.

Keep a cool head

Not everyone will agree with your views and opinions. Even if you are talking to people you don't know personally and haven't met, they are still <u>real people with feelings</u>. Don't laugh or swear at them – **be respectful** whenever you are responding to someone else's opinion. If you disagree, don't make it personal.

If something makes you angry, take time to **cool down** first before commenting. Go for a walk, make a hot drink. **THINK** – do you really need to post or comment on this?

Don't pile in

If someone else is saying something you think is mean or ridiculous, it might be quick and easy to join in on a thread of comments criticizing them, without thinking first. But **all the comments add up,** and while you might instantly forget your casual dig, the person being bombarded with them might not.

Hey! It was just one silly comment!

We've all said things we don't mean, or that came out wrong. If you say something you regret, **apologize** as soon as possible and **delete** the post or comment, if you can.

Read only

One of the best ways to stay out of arguments online is to choose to say nothing. You DON'T have to give your opinion on every single photo, or be a part of every discussion. **It's fine NOT to join in with drama on social media.** Not only does it mean you come off looking better, it's a lot less stressful.

There is NO universal 'right to free speech' on social media

Different apps have different rules about what **is** and **isn't** allowed, and some countries have laws that regulate what is acceptable to say on social media.

The bottom line is, you CAN'T say racist, homophobic, transphobic, sexist or threatening things online and expect to get away with it. DON'T use any language, even if you think it is casual or 'everyday', that you know is derogatory, discriminatory or offensive. DON'T share something upsetting either, even if it's to say "look how awful this is".

Staying within the law

It's not difficult to avoid a visit from the police if you remember to act and treat people online in the same way you would in real life.

How **NOT** to get in trouble:

☑ DON'T break the law.

☑ DON'T video yourself breaking the law.

☑ DON'T post a video online of you breaking the law.

Even if you have a made-up name and a cartoon avatar, and even if you hide your face in a photo or video, everything you post and share online leaves digital footprints back to **YOU** as a real person, which the police can follow if they need to. A criminal can be easily caught after bragging about their crime on social media.

No creeps, please

Taking photos and videos of someone **without their consent** (permission) while they are in a private place where they don't expect to be watched is ILLEGAL. Private places include locker rooms, bathrooms, bedrooms and dressing rooms.

It's a simple rule:

If you don't think this person would want a photo or video taken of them, **DON'T DO IT**. This also includes anyone too young or otherwise unable to give consent.

What did I agree to?

Sometimes people give their consent for a photo or video to be <u>taken</u>, but NOT for that image or video to be <u>shared, sent to anyone else, or put online</u>. If that image or video is of a sexual nature then you could be in **very big trouble** if you distribute it. It's not just cruel – sharing naked or sexual images of children (anyone under 18 in most countries) can mean you're guilty of distributing images of child abuse, even if it's a photo or video of one of your mates.

See **Chapter 14** for more about this.

Don't go stirring

When so many people are on social media, it's often not difficult to track down someone who has been in the press, and the opportunity to speak to them may be tempting.

Don't you get covered in poop every day?

The_B1rdman99

Great interview in 'Clean Beak' magazine, I'd love to know more.

Birdman, I just saw you on TV!

I think it's silly to have so many birds!

Commenting with your opinion could influence other people's views of them, especially if they have been linked to a police investigation or court case. **Every comment adds up,** and before you know it, you and others might be taking part in victim-blaming, or making false accusations, and ultimately **damaging someone else's reputation.** This is called **defamation,** and you could be sued for it.

Whatever someone's involvement, **YOU don't know ALL the facts,** <u>so don't pass judgement</u> on them on social media. There have been cases of trials having to be stopped or abandoned because juries have become **biased** (unfairly favouring one side), based on opinions posted by the public online.

If you threaten someone else or suggest they should be harmed, **even if you don't really mean it,** other people may decide to carry out your suggestion and then you could be convicted of **inciting violence.** Copying what someone else is saying on social media, or posting something for a 'joke', is NOT an excuse.

You could:

- be KICKED OUT of school
- LOSE your job
- or even be ARRESTED for something stupid you have posted online.

MinotaurQue5ta

Is he for real?

Al3x-the-great3st

Just ignore it. It's not worth the hassle.

MinotaurQue5ta

I can't just say nothing. You can't say stuff like that about someone.

Al3x-the-great3st

Yeah actually if you report him they should take his post down.

MinotaurQue5ta

I've got this whole response planned in my head...

Al3x-the-great3st

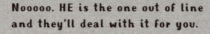

Nooooo. HE is the one out of line and they'll deal with it for you.

Chapter 6

Online bullying

The online world can feel like a more private space than the 'real' world, especially if your parents, guardians or other adults are not on your social media. Feeling that their behaviour is not being supervised can bring out the <u>worst</u> in people. Some hide behind a made-up name and avatar to say nasty things to someone that they **wouldn't dare say to their face,** while others choose to be horrible via private (direct) messages, confident that no one else will see what they have written.

When meanness and cruelty are directed at someone in particular over a period of time, that's **bullying**.

Whoever they are and whatever they say, if someone <u>deliberately</u> keeps making you feel uncomfortable, upset or embarrassed online or offline, it's all bullying, and **you DON'T have to put up with it.**

Um, was that deliberate?

Everyone can be mean sometimes, and people can act in a bullying way without realizing it. Even your own friend might do something horrible, such as purposefully sharing something that you really wouldn't want anyone else to know or see, or posting something that they think is funny, even if it's very much **NOT** funny for you.

If you feel bullied by someone you've never had a problem with before, try talking to them about it in person, or send them a private message on the app. Let them know that you **feel hurt** and ask them to **delete their post.** It might feel scary, but you could find the problem easier to solve than you think.

Was it something I said?

Someone might make a snide comment about you online to get their own back for **YOU** upsetting **THEM.** You don't want to have a public falling out on social media, so if it turns out you did do something that hurt someone's feelings, <u>apologize</u>. Then, hopefully, you can both delete your offending posts.

If you don't think you did anything wrong, discuss it in person if you can. Misunderstandings can easily happen when you're typing on the go, especially if the app you're using has a character limit.

You could post something nice about the other person to show that you're really on their side.

xo.Marnie33.xo
Talulah-Mae, you have always been THE BEST! ♥

Drive-by bullying

Some people will act in a bullying way even if you are perfectly nice to them, or you don't even know them. They might say racist, homophobic, sexist, derogatory or rude things, or go around destroying things others have built in online building games. These **bullies** like to provoke a reaction and enjoy seeing how their words and actions can upset people.

CRUSH!

SMASH!

They often bully more than one person at once, which is why they thrive on social media, scattering insults everywhere and seeing who reacts. This type of online bullying is known as (trolling).

If you get a random trolling comment on social media, the best thing to do is **ignore it**, so that you're not giving the trolls the attention they want. Hopefully they will get bored of not getting a reaction and move on.

There's more on dealing with trolls in **Chapter 8**.

Getting personal

If you're being bullied over time, it's more likely to be by someone you know, which is when advice such as "Ignore it and it will go away" probably won't work. Some adults mistakenly dismiss online bullying as less important or hurtful than bullying that happens face-to-face. Actually, online bullying can be **WORSE**, because you can't just go home from school and shut the door. It follows you wherever you go, whenever you turn on your phone.

Why do people bully?

There are lots of reasons, but people who bully often do it because:

- They are jealous of you, and don't want you to feel good.

- They feel powerful being able to make someone else feel bad.

- They are trying to turn a bully's attention from themselves to someone else.

- They feel insecure about themselves or their lives, and want to take it out on someone.

NONE of these reasons justifies bullying, but it helps to remember that a bully's behaviour is <u>their</u> responsibility. **You didn't ask for it or cause it to happen to you.**

Could YOU be a bully?

Sometimes you might find yourself doing cruel things without realizing it. Perhaps you're feeling bad about something and made fun of someone else as a distraction. Or you shared a funny meme using a photo of someone, without really caring about how they might feel about it.

If you share or join in on something mean online, that's still bullying, even if you didn't start it. Remember, behind that embarrassing photo, video or post is a **REAL PERSON WITH FEELINGS.** No one wants it to happen to them, so think about others before you post or share on social media.

Sometimes online bullying gets **VERY PERSONAL**, involving sexual information, images or videos. If you share this kind of content, or make threats to someone online, you could be <u>convicted of a crime.</u>

See **Chapter 14** for more about this, and how to get help if you are in this situation.

Online bullies can be creative in how they upset someone.

They might:

Send UNPLEASANT private messages

Post PERSONAL or EMBARRASSING things in public

Spread LIES

Face-to-face bullying and online bullying often go hand-in-hand, making you feel trapped.

It's important to remember **it's not your fault.** You are NOT responsible for someone else's nasty, cruel behaviour. And you are NOT powerless against it.

Leave me alone!

DON'T delete any bullying private messages, and **take screenshots** of bullying posts. When you have evidence to present to an adult, the bully won't be able to deny it when they are confronted.

Speaking up

If someone is making your life miserable, then **you need to find help.** Sharing what you are going through with an adult you trust is a good first step. They can help you take practical steps to make things better.

Grandpa, can we talk?

Of course.

Speak to whoever you feel comfortable with – whether that's a parent, older sibling, carer, family member, teacher, activity coach, or other adult you know and trust in person. You might also be able to talk to a school counsellor – someone who's trained to listen to and help people with difficult feelings.

You might not feel comfortable telling anyone you know about the bullying, but **YOUR** feelings **AND mental health** are just as important as anyone else's. **NO ONE** deserves to be bullied, and speaking out might help others who are also being bullied online.

#helpline

If you feel there isn't anyone you can bear to talk to, call a

BULLYING HELPLINE.

There are links to helplines on **Usborne Quicklinks** (see page 4). Some of them are open 24 hours a day.

Adults don't always have the answers straightaway, and sometimes they can suggest things that seem straightforward to them, such as:

"Avoid social media"

which, realistically, might not be that easy. Avoiding social media can feel like trying not to use your phone or the internet at all.

Even so, it can **really help to talk** about it with an adult who's on your side, and <u>together</u> you can work out a solution.

I feel lost.

Let's take this step by step.

It's good to talk

You might be tempted to try to deal with a problem on your own so that others don't think you're being overdramatic or exaggerating. **But if it's a problem for YOU, it's <u>SERIOUS</u>,** and having someone else listen to you can take the weight off your shoulders. Talking through a problem with other people can also give you a new perspective, and help you come up with strategies for coping.

Getting it all out

Bottling up bad thoughts and feelings can make them **WORSE**, because they go round and round in your head until you can't think of anything else, and they become **the BIGGEST thing in your life.**

When you don't feel in control of a situation, it's easy to turn feelings of anger and frustration onto other people, and it's even easier to take bad feelings out on yourself.

We've all blamed ourselves for something that wasn't our fault, just to feel like we're doing something about it. But punishing yourself only adds to your bad feelings. **Looking after** and **valuing yourself** is the answer to getting back in control.

Turn the page to find some good ways to get some of those feelings out, to **help you feel BETTER...**

CONTINUED...

Here are a few ways to use your anger **POSITIVELY,** so you don't have to take it out on the people in your life:

<u>Exercise:</u> kickboxing, punching pillows, dancing, running outside, swimming or anything that gets the blood pumping and muscles working releases chemicals that help to **CALM** you.

<u>Creativity:</u> writing stories, drawing, even just **SCRIBBLING** black lines all over a journal is a great way to channel your frustration.

<u>Keep a journal:</u> write down your feelings. You could even just write **ANGRY WORDS** all over the page.

Use your imagination:

there's a technique called visualization that you can use. Picture your bad thoughts as clouds in the sky and imagine them floating away. (It can take some practice.)

Focus on your strengths:

doing activities that you're **GOOD** at can help you feel better about yourself.

Reach out to other people who are being bullied:

knowing that there are other people in the same boat can remind you that you're **NOT ALONE**, and there's nothing wrong with you.

When the feelings get REALLY bad

Sometimes when people get overwhelmed with bad feelings they can't see a way out and have urges to hurt or even kill themselves. If you ever feel like this, **please, <u>PLEASE</u>**...

TALK TO SOMEONE.

You are...

valuable,
loved,
and you deserve to be
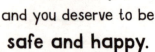

safe and happy.

There is more information about getting help for bad feelings in **Chapter 17**.

The important thing is <u>you shouldn't ever feel alone</u>, because there is **ALWAYS** someone out there who will listen to you and want to help, wherever you may be. You might be surprised at how many people have been through a tough time themselves, and are willing to help others to get back on track.

Al3x-the-great3st

Is it me, or is that post saying what I think it is?

MissT.Surfer

What's she got against you? She's always making little digs like that.

Al3x-the-great3st

It's really getting me down. I don't know what to do.

MissT.Surfer

Have you tried talking to her? I know it's awkward, but worth it?

Al3x-the-great3st

Yeah I did half-joke about it being hurtful and she just sneered.

MissT.Surfer

I think you should talk to Mr Abbot. He's really nice, and helpful.

Chapter 7

Famous faces

Just like you and your friends, many celebrities and famous people – scientists, authors, sportspeople and so on – are also on social media. They might have a private account for sharing with their close friends, as well as a public-facing account to post updates for their fans.

THEREAL_MAX_ZOOM

Celebrity account

MARTYJONES1987

Private account

Stars can post photos and videos on social media as they go about their day and know that their posts will get lots of attention.

15 mins ago **MaxZoomMUSICofficial**

> **" Just wolfing down some brekkie before recording this morning 👍 "**

3 mins ago Lulu&l
Scrambled eggs are my favourite!!

5 mins ago Petey_Man338
You have to try them with brown sauce, Max.

11 mins ago Jojo_in_thehouse
Oooh does this mean a new album soon?

Social media allows you an insight into the lives of famous people who you wouldn't otherwise have the chance to meet. It's also **good marketing** for celebrities to have a public online presence: by being on social media they are able to talk about and promote their work directly to their fans.

Do we have a connection?

Instead of being caught off-guard by fans whilst doing their weekly shop, famous people can use social media to post statements which will reach lots of people at once.

Stars are unlikely to disable comments on their public-facing apps, as they want useful feedback from their fans, but just because you CAN talk to them, doesn't mean you HAVE to. You're not an interviewer and they have a right not to respond to lots of questions.

They certainly can't reply to every single message they get sent.

Not now.

Lulu&I **Why did you dump Pascal?**

Lulu&I **What's Bee-Z REALLY like?**

Lulu&I **Do you like pineapples?**

Lulu&I is typing...

Although a famous person's public account shows more of their life than you can find out in the news, they still have a right to privacy regarding all the information they DON'T post. Having a public social media account is another **part of their job** and they work as hard at maintaining their public persona as you do. That persona might not even be the 'real' them at all, and they might even have publicists to post updates for them if they are too busy.

3 mins ago ThePOPsiclesOfficial

" Having SO MUCH FUN playing for you all tonight! ♪♪ "

Use your voice wisely

Social media is a great place to find out what lots of people are thinking and talking about, so even people such as MPs and company CEOs have an account, so they can connect with a wide audience and get feedback.

Social media provides a great opportunity to be able to give your opinion and suggestions to people who can do something about it.

BUT, remember to **talk to others online as <u>politely</u> as you would in person.** Everything you post online adds to your reputation, and you never know where you might end up applying for a job in the future...

Social media stars

Some ordinary people become so well known on social media that they can make a career out of it. These people are usually **bloggers, vloggers,** or **photographers.**

Bloggers are people who have a website page (a blog) on which they write about their lives, or talk about a certain topic they are interested in. They can promote their blog on social media: talking to their readers, and attracting more.

TAP, TAP

TAP, TAP

BookBlogger

Vloggers are video bloggers. They do the same as bloggers, but via video — a vlog. Vloggers post videos on a popular subject and gain lots of subscribers, who watch all their videos. Some vloggers don't even edit their videos, and instead choose to livestream their talks, activities or reviews.

Testing 'Sparkle Beauty' make-up today folks...

Livestreaming whilst talking about a game you are playing is very popular with gaming fans.

Collectively, these people are known as (**content-creators**) – the blogs they write, videos they film and photos they take are all 'content' that other people like to read or view.

Popular content-creators **earn money from advertisers,** who pay to advertise next to their posts and profile. Becoming well known enough to attract lots of fans and advertisers, AND posting enough content to keep that interest and income, often makes being a social media professional a full-time job.

Social media content-creators specialize in a certain area, based on their skills, interests and current trends.

Some popular areas of interest include:

ART & CRAFTING:
how-to videos and tutorials, restoring or repurposing items, designing and making

BEAUTY:
hair styling, make-up

COMPUTER GAMES:
reviewing, playing - often livestreaming

FASHION:
modern, vintage and handmade clothing

FITNESS

FOOD:
cooking, baking, healthy eating, special diets, recipes

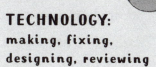

TECHNOLOGY:
making, fixing, designing, reviewing

TRAVEL:
photography, reviews

PING!

11:03

NEW VIDEO from
BettyBakesBread

The more frequently content-creators post on social media, the more people will see their work and possibly like or comment on it. Fans can subscribe or follow, which means they will get notified when new content is posted.

Today, we're using Quick's Flour.

As the number of views, followers and subscribers grows, the content-creator's posts spread further across social media and attract even more people, along with the attention of advertisers.

MY RECOMMENDATIONS

Many content-creators post reviews of products in their area of expertise. Those who become successful are described as influencers, which means the people who follow them online may be persuaded to buy any products they use or mention. Influencers are very attractive to advertisers, and successful ones can earn a lot of money.

So you want to be famous online?

Influencers are often referred to as 'personalities'. ANYONE with a social media account can try to become a social media influencer... which means it's **very competitive,** with LOTS of people trying to attract the attention of the same fans. Below are some of the personal qualities that help vloggers, bloggers and photographers draw people's attention, and some that don't.

witty   passionate

quirky   chatty   insightful

versus

confrontational   offensive

arrogant   judgemental

DON'T try this at home

There is a 'stunt' trend on social media where people video or livestream themselves doing <u>DANGEROUS</u> things. These exciting-looking videos often attract lots of views, but sadly a number of them end in **serious injury** or even **DEATH.** Trying to copy someone else's stunt yourself is no less dangerous, whether you are filming it or not.

That's crazy!

Look at this!

Being a popular social media personality is <u>NOT</u> worth your life, or the life of someone who tries to copy you.

Don't take risks just to impress a faceless online audience.

Eek! I don't want people looking at <u>ME</u>!

I'm shy...

Although creating public content on social media is all about **engaging your audience,** you don't have to have a stand-out public persona if your content is interesting enough. You don't have to use your REAL name on your professional page or profile, and depending on your area of expertise, you could choose to show only your hands in videos, or not talk at all and put your videos to music instead.

As a content-creator, it's even more important **NOT** to put <u>personal information</u> on your profile, as your followers and subscribers will mostly be people you don't know.

Be careful!

Once you post something online, **you don't have control** over how and to whom it might spread. Your face is even more personal to you than your real name, so think carefully about whether you want to put it onto a public-facing app for anyone to see, replay, edit or share at any time.

No one wants their serious presentation re-released with a silly filter added!

Sounds great?

Although being paid to share your hobby or talent with others online might <u>sound</u> like your ideal job, there are other **potential drawbacks** to being a social media personality:

- People who earn money through social media still have to pay taxes. If social media were your main job, you'd need to register as self-employed and keep track of your accounts.

- You might become a target for online trolls who forget that anyone in the public eye is a real person with feelings.

- As your posts become more popular, you could become obsessed with the number of likes, followers or subscribers you have.

REFRESH...REFRESH...**REFRESH**...

Phew!

BATTERY LOW

Work, work, work...

Being an influencer or social media personality is a **LOT** of **hard work** - your fans will expect you to create and post new content regularly, to keep up to date with trends in your area of expertise, and to engage with their comments and suggestions.

It's not worth your time responding to critics and trolls, and even replying to supportive messages could quickly become tiring. Spending so much time trying to be unique or special can feel overwhelming, as can constant comparison with other influencers.

You have to be ready to **protect your wellbeing and mental health** when you 'put yourself out there' on social media.

See **Chapter 17** for more information on looking after your mental health.

MinotaurQue5ta

I love my knitted dragon! Thank you so much, You're so talented!!

MissT.Surfer

Haha, yeah my sister says I should get a website or blog or something.

MinotaurQue5ta

You should do some videos showing how you make them!

MissT.Surfer

Er, not sure I want to be on camera???

MinotaurQue5ta

I would LOVE to do social media vids for a living. So glam.

MissT.Surfer

Nah. It'd take SO LONG to edit, there'd be no time to make stuff!

Chapter 8

Online trolls

Some people might want to join social media to escape who they are in 'real life', make entirely new friends or create an online persona that is very different to their real-world personality. Some use a made-up name and avatar to feel **anonymous** online, and think no one will find out who they really are.

> My superpower is invisibility, HAHA!

This feeling of anonymity can lead some people to act in a mean way that they wouldn't in real life. Those who take the opportunity to be deliberately horrible online to people they don't know are called **trolls.**

A target of trolls

Trolls often latch onto public figures or someone who has been in the news. They also tend to throw around racist, sexist, homophobic and transphobic insults. They post these **offensive** and **personal** comments, often repeatedly, in order to attract attention, stir up bad feeling, and provoke reactions.

They might:

- Find it amusing to **CAUSE TROUBLE**, and wind other people up so they can watch an argument.

- Want **PUBLIC ATTENTION** from well-known people, and think being nasty to them will gain a response.

- **FEEL INSECURE** and take out their anger on people who seem happy and confident.

- Get a **SENSE OF POWER** in making other people feel bad, or...

- They might not give much thought to how the target of their nastiness feels at all.

One thing trolls **ALL** have in common is the belief that <u>by hiding their name and face,</u> <u>they can get away with being abusive online.</u>

Troll psychology

There are a few reasons why trolls think they can get away with what they do:

1. They think if they are anonymous, there won't be any consequences for their actions. They won't be confronted in person by whoever they are trolling, so there is no risk to themselves and they have nothing to lose by acting however they like. Trolls might feel 'freer' online because of this.

No one knows it is me...

2. They feel there is safety in numbers. When they see others trolling, they join in or start trolling themselves. They think their nasty comment is just one of many, so it's no big deal and people should just get used to it being part of social media life.

3. Trolls feel encouraged if people don't challenge them. They think their horrible opinion is held by the majority and that they are speaking for a large number of people.

It's not hard to see why trolls are such a **problem** on social media.

Why me?

If you find yourself attracting the attention of a troll, **DON'T TAKE IT PERSONALLY.** Trolls are <u>indiscriminate bullies</u> who like to take chances and see who reacts. Some people are trolled for the way they look, their sexuality, their religion, where they live, or how much money they have. BUT it's never really because of those things, it's because trolls have time on their hands and an internet connection. They may move on as quickly as they appeared.

Shaking them off

Trolls attract more trolls, so replying to one will only draw attention to their pointless messages. They can be **VERY difficult to ignore,** though, especially if there is more than one troll targeting the same person.

FLING

DON'T WORRY

as there are some things you can do about trolls...

CONTINUED...

BLOCKING

All social media apps have a feature where you can block someone from seeing and commenting on your account or profile. You can sometimes spot a troll before they say anything. If someone's username is something racist, sexist, homophobic or otherwise offensive, BLOCK THEM before they have a chance to strike.

REPORTING

On most social media apps, ANYONE can report a user for making trolling comments, even if those comments are directed towards someone else. That means if you see trolling happening, YOU can do something about it. (And if you make trolling comments yourself, anyone who reads those comments could report YOU for it.)

SPEAKING OUT

There is strength in numbers, and in speaking out against trolling. Some well-known organizations, such as football clubs, have announced the closure of their social media accounts, to show they won't tolerate online abuse and the rest of social media shouldn't either. You could start a petition or movement to drown out the trolls.

Trolls can be persistent and incessant. Many people who are trolled suffer from poor mental health as a result, and some are driven off social media permanently.

If this is happening to YOU, there are more tips for how to deal with it in **Chapter 17**.

I think I've been **doxxed**!

Oh no! ...Er, what's that?

'Doxxing' is when a troll finds out and publicly posts real–life personal information about someone online, such as their address, often in order to encourage others to harass them. In some countries this is illegal, so if it happens to you, you might have to involve the police.

And obviously,
<u>**NEVER** do it yourself!</u>

Making violent threats online is **ALWAYS ILLEGAL.** If someone is harassing you in this way, <u>report it to the police</u>.

 # Oops, I trolled

If you see someone or something online that you don't like, you might be tempted to make an angry or mean comment. It might make you feel good in the moment, and you might quickly forget about it, but your upsetting comment will stay there for all to see.

Making a thoughtless comment to someone you don't know is silly, but if you find yourself deliberately saying something nasty to a stranger to cause them distress, you're in danger of becoming a troll.

127

What you write on social media affects the people who read it. Celebrities and other public figures – politicians, key workers, broadcasters etc – are **REAL PEOPLE,** who have **feelings** that can be hurt. Before you post a mean comment, think how you would feel being called those names and having complete strangers be nasty to <u>YOU</u>.

If you think you might have trolled someone, it's not too late to do something about it. Delete your horrible comments and apologize.

Remember, if you don't have anything positive to say to someone then...

<u>DON'T</u>
COMMENT AT ALL!

Chapter 9

Your money and social media

You might not think your social media use relates to how you spend your money, but when you click on an advert,  or download a free game, you might find yourself paying out when you didn't expect to. There are also scams to watch out for, plus sponsorship and donation requests.

Not to mention buying and selling on social media... it can be hard to keep track of your money!

I only went online to update my profile picture!

So many adverts

Social media platforms and apps are free to use because they are funded by advertising. Adverts may appear on your feed, in a dedicated area of the app, or as pop-ups , which are small windows that suddenly appear on your screen.

Unlike adverts in the local paper, adverts on social media are usually 'targeted'. This means the adverts you see are based on your **age, location, gender** and any other information about yourself that you might be giving away on your profile, such as your **hobbies** and **interests**.

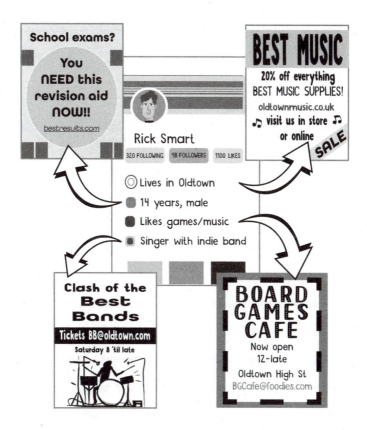

Targeted adverts can also be based on your previous online purchases, pages you have liked and your [**browser history**], which is the record of the websites you have recently visited. Advertisers get this information from website [**cookies**], which track your activity on each site.

That's why you might find
adverts for the shoes you
were looking at online
start to follow you

Here's what
you wanted.

around on your social media.
The internet isn't reading your mind,
it's just watching and taking notes.

Although it's annoying to have text about
cookies appear on almost every site you
visit, it's important to not just close the
pop-up window, or click 'ACCEPT' to get
rid of it as quickly as possible. You could be
allowing your data to be collected and even
sold on to other interested companies.

Make sure you read through the text
and click 'REJECT ALL' or choose the
information you are willing to let the site
collect, and then click 'SAVE PREFERENCES'.

Ignore any tempting adverts for a payday loan, or 'Buy now, pay later' deals for buying that guitar you want. The high interest rates charged on payday loans require you to <u>pay back much more</u> than you actually borrow and, along with 'pay later' offers, this can end up causing you a lot of **STRESS** and get you into **SERIOUS TROUBLE.**

See Usborne Quicklinks (page 4) if you need help with this.

Ad blockers

There are free ad blockers that you can download, BUT research them carefully to make sure they will <u>only block the ads you actually want blocked</u>, because some also block **useful things** such as online shopping baskets and ticket booking websites.

Some blockers allow you to 'untick' features like these that you don't want blocked, along with certain websites that you are willing to allow adverts from, to support that website's income from advertising.

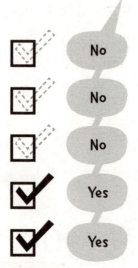

No

No

No

Yes

Yes

Is this a scam?

Scammers aim to get people's money or personal information. You might read news articles about older people being scammed out of their bank details or conned by an online advert, and think that couldn't happen to you because you're tech-savvy. But really, **it can happen to anyone,** as online scams become more sophisticated and thrive on social media.

Turn the page for different types of **social media scams** and how to AVOID them...

EMAILED DIRECT FROM THE DESK OF

Honest John's Bank

We're the bank to trust...

SCAM ALERT!

FAKE JOB ADVERTS

These may advertise jobs paid in cash, and suggest they are 'quick', 'easy' or 'local'. They may ask you to fill in personal details, ask for an upfront admin or joining fee, or ask to see documents proving your identity. They may also suggest direct messaging you with more details, or ask you to call a premium rate number.

IS THIS
➡ YOUR ⬇
DREAM
JOB?
· FABULOUS hourly rates!
· Work from ANYWHERE!
· FLEXIBLE hours!
· BRILLIANT bonus!
Don't miss out!
* APPLY TODAY *
JUST send your name & bank details
to dreamjobs@mail.com

One 'quick, easy' job advert asks you to accept money into your bank account, then transfer it back to the job advertiser, for which they would pay you a small fee. They may imply this is to save them paying too much tax, but it's actually money laundering, which is <u>ILLEGAL!</u>

! Avoid job adverts with poor spelling and grammar, and where the contact is using a personal email address. Don't click the links in any job adverts or communication until you have researched the company to check they really exist.

! Legitimate companies won't ask you for any bank details before you have started the job.

! Be suspicious of being 'headhunted' or any personalized job offers from agencies you haven't signed up with. Don't agree to direct message or meet up with anyone you don't know. If in doubt, check out the company website and call them for more information.

SCAM ALERT!

'URGENT ACTION REQUIRED'

These scams can take many forms – perhaps a pop-up saying you have won something and have a certain amount of time to enter your bank details to claim your prize, or a message saying your login details have been hacked or are about to expire and you need to re-enter them as soon as possible. The aim is to PANIC you into acting QUICKLY. These are called 'phishing' scams.

Phishing scammers send messages pretending to be from reputable companies to fool people into revealing personal and financial information. They can copy logos and company email addresses, but there will usually be typos, layout issues, or other non-professional aspects of the message that should alert you to it being a scam.

! Legitimate companies WON'T
ask you to confirm any <u>financial</u>
or <u>login</u> information via email.

! If the message asks you to call a number,
look it up online or call the official
company number listed online instead.

! Be wary of any messages saying you have
won a prize. You will almost certainly NOT
have won anything.

! Check the details of the message and
the sender carefully, DON'T RUSH.

SCAM ALERT!

CLICKBAIT

Clickbait articles have an attention-grabbing headline that makes you want to click on it to read more. These are often just clever marketing ploys to boost a website's traffic, but sometimes they are scams. Clickbait scams may:

- Ask you to download some software to view the full article, which actually installs malware on your device.

- Appear as a message from a friend saying there is a photo of you online that you need to click the link to see, or an advert saying you can check who has viewed your profile.

These links then direct you to a fake social media page to steal your login details.

YOU HAVE WON!

! Adverts for quizzes and questionnaires can also look like fun, but they may ask you to input your phone number to get the results, where you will be subscribed to a premium text service without your knowledge.

! Be wary of free app downloads, which may ask you to input personal details, or install malware.

! Avoid clicking on links that have shortened URLs (probably made up of capital letters and numbers), which don't show the full web address of the page you are being directed to.

! Don't use social media on a shared device or public wi-fi network, otherwise others might be abe to see your information.

BITCOIN INVESTMENTS

Scammers often like to be paid in
(Bitcoin). They can offer to double
your Bitcoin if you invest with them,
or perhaps offer to exchange your Bitcoin
for cash. Phishing scammers impersonate
the Bitcoin brand themselves. <u>There's almost
always a too-good-to-be-true link to click</u>.

Unless you are already <u>very confident</u> with
Bitcoin and know your way around these
kinds of scams, it's easier to avoid getting
involved with it on social media.

This looks
ALMOST like the
real thing...

THINK!

! DON'T put personal or contact information on social media.

! NEVER send money or give your bank details to someone you don't know in person, and don't give your PIN number to ANYONE.

! Make sure your privacy settings are HIGH so that random strangers can't message you.

Stealth marketing

Often people like to read reviews or get recommendations from friends before they hand over their money – they don't trust advertisers as much as 'real' people. If you spend a lot of time following social media influencers and other professionals, you may come to trust their views and opinions as much as those of your own friends.

That makes influencers very attractive to advertisers. Many brands send influencers free products in the hope that they will like and recommend them to their audience, which is stealth, or indirect, marketing.

A LITTLE SOMETHING FOR YOU. WE HOPE YOU LIKE IT.

FROM

Shakin' Shakes

Mmm, I love my daily Coffee-Inna-Cup.

I'd never drink coffee.

COFFEE INNA CUP

Sometimes, however, brands pay influencers to recommend a product, which is called 'paid product promotion'. Some countries have laws that say influencers must make it clear to their audience that they are being paid for a recommendation, but it's not universal.

It's fine to take recommendations from influencers and other professionals on social media, but bear in mind they may be prioritizing trying to **sell something**, so ask yourself if this might be a paid-for ad.

Also, make sure to look at online reviews and ask your friends in order to get the best picture of whether a product or service is worth investing in.

In-game purchases

Many free games are advertised on social media, which you can download and play on your phone, as well as on dedicated social gaming sites. Although they are 'free', the games are designed to encourage you to **pay out money.** When you sign up to play, you are asked to register a bankcard if you haven't already. Just as the game is getting exciting, a pop-up will ask you if you want to access more levels, win back lives, or buy new objects.

You might find yourself clicking the 'buy now' button, without stopping to think about the cost. This can result in some serious expense, and there are stories of people spending huge amounts on their bankcards, without even realizing they've paid out **REAL** money.

Even in games that aren't free, or you pay a subscription to play, there are often options to **buy gaming advantages,** or **unlock special features.** If you think about it, this isn't very fair on players who can't afford to pay for extras. If a game is unfair, it's probably not as much fun to play, and if you pay for an advantage, you can't be proud of your gaming success being down to your own hard work and skill.

When you sign up to play a game, if you register a pre-paid card, with a **SET AMOUNT** of money, you'll <u>NEVER</u> go over your limit. On some apps you can also turn off in-game purchases, in the menu under 'settings'.

That's a good idea!

Just one more...

Once you start to pay to unlock extras in a game, **it can become hard to stop.** Some games offer a pay-for 'lucky dip' element, where you could win (pay for) nothing special, or an in-game reward.

CLICK & WIN ANOTHER LIFE...

CLICK

JUST **ONE** COIN TO PLAY

YES! I have 4 in a row! I'm feeling lucky...

148

These offers could pop up time and time again while you play, and even if they don't cost much, **you can find yourself becoming addicted to paying out,** and end up spending a lot of money. Addictive

games like this don't usually have an age limit, and they don't fall under the remit of gambling laws.

Remember,

these games are designed to **make the DEVELOPERS money** through enticing pop-ups and offers. So THINK CAREFULLY about whether you are willing to be sucked in.

Buying and selling

Some social media apps have pages where you can buy and sell things, in an informal way. You should be able to find details of how to do this in the app's 'help' pages, but there are some **general things to remember when buying and selling online:**

Buying

TELL AN ADULT about what you are planning to buy, and let them see your messages with the seller. (And don't get drawn into messages about anything other than the item you are buying.) That way, you have help on hand if the seller makes unwanted contact with you at any time.

ALWAYS USE A SECURE INTERNET CONNECTION when shopping online — avoid using public wi-fi — so that others can't access your financial details.

DON'T PAY BY BANK TRANSFER. Try to pay online through a reputable payment site or ask a parent or guardian if you can use their credit card. That way you have buyer protection if the seller doesn't send your item. (If you're asked if you want to 'save' your card details, play safe and tick 'no'.)

If the seller is local, **DON'T GO BY YOURSELF** to pay or pick up the item, take an adult with you.

Er, will it fit?!

Dad, it's fiiiiine.

Selling

Make sure you DON'T APPEAR IN ANY PHOTOS of the item you are selling.

Remember to factor in the COST OF POSTAGE in the price.

If your item is collection-only, DON'T GIVE THE BUYER YOUR ADDRESS UNTIL THEY HAVE BOUGHT THE ITEM. Arrange a time for the buyer to pick it up, when an adult will be at home with you. If the buyer turns up unannounced and you are on your own, don't let them in. Rearrange for a more convenient time.

If a buyer or seller harasses or upsets you, REPORT IT through the app and tell an adult.

Good will

Requests for donations and sponsorship appear all the time on social media, usually through, or forwarded by, your friends. There are **many genuine sites** through which you can sponsor someone, or donate to a good cause or (crowdsourcing) campaign. If you want to give your money in this way, ALWAYS CHECK that the link you have been sent is from a reputable site.

Save the ORANGUTANS

TheRightJackson

Whoop whoop, only gone and WON some new headphones!

Eva&Aardvark

Whaaaat? How?

TheRightJackson

Being the 100th visitor to the URStore4Tech site.

Eva&Aardvark

Oh those pop-up things are dodgy, don't click on them!

TheRightJackson

They only wanted my email address...

Eva&Aardvark

Unsubscribe from their emails or they'll try to get your bank deets!

Chapter 10

Health and fitness marketing

If you've ever bought some sports kit or searched for a smoothie recipe online, you'll probably start to find things popping up on your social media. It might be adverts and posts from fitness trainers, diet 'gurus' and many others in the health or fitness business, **all promising to change the way you LOOK and FEEL.**

PING!

PING!

PING!

New offer!

PING!

PING!

Start your fitness journey TODAY!

JOIN

Ditch the diet. Try our NEW meal plan!

SIGN UP

Look beautiful, feel great! START NOW!

ACCEPT

Promotions for a healthier lifestyle may seem innocent

enough. However, with beauty and fashion brands, and celebrity influencers also recommending products and services to improve your 'lifestyle', this stream of advice can feel like **one continuous advert for a better way of living**

– one that requires your ongoing dedication and <u>YOUR MONEY</u>.

Before you sign up to the latest product or service that promises to 'change your life', make sure you **do your research** and THINK CAREFULLY about what would <u>really</u> make you feel happier and healthier.

156

Figuring out fitness

We have the technology to record a lot about our lives – **WHERE** we are, **WHAT** we're doing and **WHO** we're doing it with, particularly when we're exercising.

There are popular wearable trackers, monitors and other 'smart tech' that can analyze your heart rate, your sweat levels, and even how well you sleep. **It's interesting...**

...but is it <u>necessary</u>? This tech is expensive and all this information can feel a little overwhelming, especially if you're not sure what it all really means, or what to do with it.

Personal training

It's important to look after your health with a **balanced diet and exercise,** but beware of adverts and forums where health

and fitness promoters claim to be able to help – telling you what's normal, what's not, and what to do about it.

Professional health and fitness advice is often advertised as 'tailored', 'bespoke' or 'one-on-one', all of which makes it EXPENSIVE, as you are paying for **an expert's undivided attention,** rather than getting tips during a gym workout or exercise class.

You might find yourself signing up to pay out money if you subscribe to various personal fitness programmes or meal plans, which might be unnecessary.

Am I nearly there yet?

If you are worried about your body in any way, tell your school nurse or counsellor how you are feeling, and they can help you get some advice.

See **Usborne Quicklinks** (page 4) for guidance on how to be more active and healthy.

What to eat

People seek out advice about what is best for them to eat for lots of different reasons – perhaps because they have **food allergies or intolerances,** they want to **lose or gain weight,** or to help them with their **fitness.** This high demand for advice on 'healthy eating' means you'll always find adverts for amazing 'new' ingredients, products and meal plans.

WONDERFUL WATERMELON NO NEED TO EAT ANYTHING ELSE!

Many of these are created or endorsed by influencers and celebrities, which gives them a sense of credibility, even if those personalities are NOT nutrition (healthy food) experts.

Influencers and celebrities <u>are often **PAID** to promote products and services</u> so, along with the fact that much of the information in this area can be confusing, **it may make you wonder who to trust.**

I play a doctor on TV, so you'll probably buy what I promote.

Whatever advice you are looking for, it's important **NOT** to mistake someone who has a lot of followers, great photos and a convincing brand name, for an expert. **Anyone can pretend to be anyone on the internet.** You don't need any medical qualifications or proof of effectiveness to set yourself up as a diet or workout guru.

Speak to your family doctor or school nurse for help finding registered dieticians, nutritionists and other health professionals.

Quick fixes

To look after your health, you need to make time for physical activity and **value your wellbeing.** Sometimes that can feel difficult, so the weight-loss industry makes money out of convincing people that losing weight is the key to improving your health, by promoting **fad diets** on social media. A 'fad diet' is a very restrictive or unbalanced diet. It's often promoted as being 'short-term' and tends to make UNREALISTIC (weight-loss) claims. Trying to follow a fad diet can make eating both boring and stressful.

Alongside fad food diets, the healthy-eating industry promotes detoxes, or **cleansing** diets and products. A 'cleanse' might sound gentle and lovely, but it's <u>unnecessary</u>, and often involves skipping meals or spending a lot of time on the toilet.

If you are concerned about your weight or body shape, talk to an adult you trust, so that someone knows how you are feeling. Attempting a quick fix is likely to be unpleasant, and if you did manage to lose or gain weight it wouldn't be for long, because **NO ONE can permanently stick to a fad or detox diet.** If you <u>take a steady approach</u> to getting fit and healthy, you're much more likely to be able to maintain a good level of health and fitness in the long-term, and less likely to develop an unhealthy relationship with food.

'As part of a healthy lifestyle'

A large part of health and fitness marketing is focused on manufactured products called **dietary supplements,** which are marketed on social media as 'essential buys' to support your body in working well.

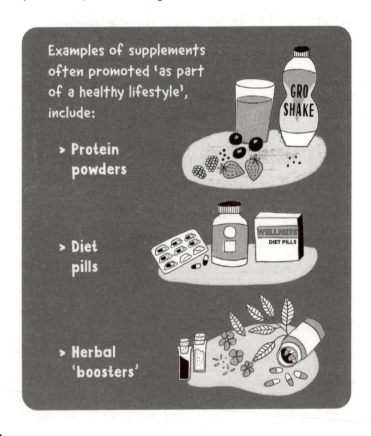

Examples of supplements often promoted 'as part of a healthy lifestyle', include:

> Protein powders

> Diet pills

> Herbal 'boosters'

In reality, these things are NOT required and **may not be harmless.** Even products marketed as 'plant-based', 'natural' or 'herbal' could be harmful, because the sale of them is often <u>unregulated</u>, which means ANYONE can make them, sell them and claim that they have 'wonderous' health and nutritional properties.

Supplements are <u>NOT</u> medicines,

and may interfere with any medicines you may be taking.

Although they should have an ingredients list, manufacturers don't have to prove what's in these products, or even that they work. So, they might give you digestive problems, and at worst **they could MAKE YOU ILL**.

Pills and supplements sold on social media could be imported from abroad and <u>may not carry any health warnings</u>, <u>or any dosage information</u>. Yet, somewhere there may be some small print that contains a **disclaimer,** which is a line saying that if this product harms you it's NOT the manufacturer's or seller's problem.

What's your motivation?

You may not be able to avoid images of glorified body types appearing on your social media feed. Adverts that use these images are designed to prompt you to compare yourself and decide you need to change your face, body or lifestyle.

You may want to get fitter and healthier for **YOU,** but then get enticed by the promise of achieving a 'better' body, or the body shape of a health and fitness promoter, and, before you know it, you are trying to achieve a certain body shape, **to impress OTHER people.**

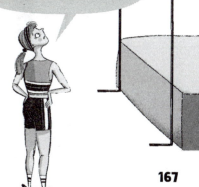

Who set this bar? I didn't. Is anyone else jumping over this?

If you find yourself **obsessing** over your workout routine or meal planning, getting overly **competitive** with yourself, or becoming **anxious** about the way you look and the progress you are making, <u>you could be at risk of hurting yourself physically or mentally with your health and fitness goals</u>. If you feel a bit out of control regarding diet and exercise, make sure you **talk to an adult you trust,** such as a school nurse or counsellor, who can help.

Joining a sports club, or going swimming or running with a friend may be all you need to **feel happy and healthy in yourself.**

Chapter 11

Achieving the perfect photo

On social media, people **LOVE** to show **what they're doing, when they're doing it,** and smartphone cameras allow people to take high-quality photos to upload while they are out and about. So, there is usually something new and interesting to see whenever you go on social media.

Is that enough? My jaw hurts!

All these eye-catching posts might make you feel like **YOU** should also be posting photos of lovely holidays, glamorous selfies and fun activities, but creating these photos might not have been as quick and easy as it looks!

With **MILLIONS** of photos being uploaded to social media daily, trying to post a photo that stands out from the crowd can get **competitive,** and may even become a bit of an <u>obsession</u>.

Trying too hard to achieve an 'effortless' or spontaneous photo can take the fun out of a holiday or hanging out with your friends, and **you don't have to record EVERY minute** of what you experience.

Instead of spending all your time thinking of the next photo opportunity, remember to actually **enjoy the moment, <u>without your phone.</u>** If you really want, you could spend time editing your photos later to get the effect you are looking for.

Hands free for other things!

Artistic and fun filters

Many apps have features that allow you to do basic editing of your photos and videos, such as **rotating** and **cropping.** In addition to this, they often give you a range of (filters) to choose from. Filters can be applied to photos and videos to create different effects, such as to make them look more stylish or humorous.

Photo filters change the light and colours in an image, to give it a different feel. Perhaps you want to make the photo look retro, or more atmospheric, to distort it, or simply to make it sharper or more stylish. There are filters to help you achieve all these effects, and turn your photo into a work of art.

You can also use filters to add graphics to your photos that look like stickers. You could add sparkly gold stars, or cartoon features, and so on.

Video filters often use animated graphics, such as exaggerated comedy features that move in tandem with the person in the video. These are augmented reality effects – digital images superimposed over a real-life video, looking like they are interacting with the real environment.

Filters are a **quick and easy tool** to liven up your photos and videos. With so many available to play around with, you don't need the latest phone, designer outfits or expensive trips to create eye-catching images. Remember, many of the perfect-looking photos filling your feed might just be the result of a filter.

Face filters

Appearance-enhancing – or 'beauty' – filters are very popular. They are designed to 'retouch' faces, and can make **teeth whiter, skin smoother,** and even **reshape facial features.** When you use a fun filter, the alterations to your photo are obvious, but most beauty filters are designed so that the viewer doesn't realize a filter has been used at all.

Let's just freshen you up...

You might want to edit your selfies to get rid of perceived blemishes, and that may make you feel **more confident and in control** when you post your selfies online.

But with SO MANY types of edits available, if you get stuck in too enthusiastically, <u>it can be hard to know where to stop</u>. You could make an edit here, there... and EVERYWHERE, and before you know it you'll have a 'selfie' that's UNRECOGNIZABLE.

BEFORE

AFTER

Oh dear! I got a bit carried away.

Don't lose sight of yourself

To some people, having an unfiltered photo of themselves on social media is <u>unthinkable</u>. But if you are using these filters daily, or on every photo, make sure you take a step back once in a while. You might find you like the **REAL you.**

You may have features you're not completely happy with. Just remember, **you're a unique person, not an off-the-shelf avatar.** When you take a selfie it is a representation of yourself, so there's no point editing out what makes you, **YOU.**

The UGLY SIDE
of beauty filters

Some of the most popular effects offered by these 'appearance-enhancing' filters are those making SKIN PALER, FACES THINNER and EYES BIGGER. These are <u>Western ideals</u> and the more popular these filters become, you may find all you see online are the same types of faces cropping up over and over again, with VERY LITTLE DIVERSITY.

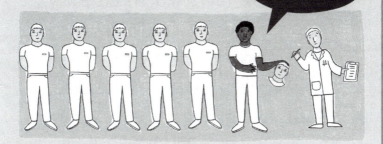

You might feel like you need to fit in, yet there are

NO fashion and beauty rules.

Start your own trend, or ignore them all completely!

Filter-free

If you can't find the effect you're looking for from a filter, and you have the time to explore and practise, you could **create a beauty look yourself.** There are plenty of beauty make-up tutorials on social media, and lots of make-up artists who can create AMAZING illusions and artwork using just make-up and their own face as a canvas. Don't be afraid to **experiment** and see where your talents might lie. You could create a unique photo in REAL LIFE, rather than using a standard filter option, and be proud of your hard work.

Photo fatigue

Most social media apps also allow advertising in some form, so alongside the sheer daily volume of other people's photo updates, there is a  **steady stream of advertising images** suggesting what you should be:

buying,

wearing

 or **doing...**

All of which could make you feel like you **just can't compete** in this portrayal of the perfect life. BUT REMEMBER, YOU DON'T **HAVE** TO!

Photos are <u>subjective</u>, which means **not everyone sees them the same way.** Something that one person thinks looks IDEAL, someone else will think looks the OPPOSITE.

If scrolling through 'perfect' photos, or trying to recreate them, causes you <u>more stress than enjoyment</u>, or you start to compare yourself to images in a NEGATIVE way...

It's time to
STOP FOLLOWING
accounts that
MAKE YOU FEEL BAD
about yourself.

Or, maybe it's time to take a break from social media completely, and spend some time **creating fun memories OFFLINE.**

Chapter 12

Body image and social media

With the fashion, beauty, health and fitness industries all posting images of perceived 'ideal' faces and bodies, plus the **carefully chosen** and **filtered** photos posted by your friends and contacts, social media can feel like one continuous beauty pageant.

Mirror, mirror, on the wall...

The sheer volume of images available makes it difficult to avoid constant comparison, which can turn us all into critics. Once you turn that critical eye on **YOURSELF,** it's often very hard to turn it away again.

Being **positive** about your body is an important aspect of having good mental health, so it's worth taking care of your body confidence as much as your physical health. If the images you see on social media are dragging your confidence down, you can bet it's happening to other people too.

What you see on social media is **NOT ALWAYS** the real thing. As you scroll through these images, it's important to be aware of **HOW** and **WHY** they were created, and just how <u>artificial</u> many of them are, so you **don't lose track of reality**.

Airbushing

Airbrushing is the process of <u>digitally altering photos</u> of people and products to 'make them look more attractive'. It is used in any industry that uses images of people – from fashion to weightlifting.

ORIGINAL

AIRBRUSHED

Advertisers use models to make products look as attractive as possible. The aim is to make people **aspire** to look like the model, and believe that they can achieve this by buying whatever is being advertised.

Photos are airbrushed not because there is anything wrong with how the model looks in real life, but to create a vision that the advertisers think is so <u>aspirational and desirable</u>, customers just **won't be able to resist handing over their money.**

Airbrushing can make even **celebrities feel insecure** – many don't have a say in whether their photos are airbrushed by the advertisers and brands they work with. Which means when celebrities step outside in the real world, they are competing with digital images of themselves that they know AREN'T REAL.

Trying to achieve the impossible

This kind of photo editing is, understandably, difficult to spot, and if you are not aware of how much of it goes on, you could easily be fooled into believing all models naturally look like they do in the photos. Advertisers DON'T CARE that a digitally-altered look is IMPOSSIBLE to achieve in real life.

In some countries there are rules around **misleading advertising,** and advertisers have to be clear that an image has been altered, but many adverts still slip through the net. If you believe someone REALLY DOES look like that, you can be convinced that look must surely be attainable by buying the advertised product. But these advertised faces and bodies might not even exist.

Advertisers can afford to spend lots of money on <u>hair, make-up, set, outfits **AND** models</u> to create a great photo, **AND THEN** to <u>digitally alter it</u>. These images can present an **irresistible goal** that people will pay to try to achieve, but also create great anxiety in people about the way they look.

Using digital technology, a designer can create an image of a person to **ANY SPECIFICATION.**

CLICK

We can make anybody have ANY body!

That's why airbrushed images are <u>NOT an achievable goal</u> for anyone in **REAL LIFE.**

Restrictive eating

Social media can create a **distorted view of reality,** one that can affect your own view of yourself (and anyone's view of themselves, including celebrities). Comments from random trolls, fears of being tagged in unflattering photos, or even lack of likes for your favourite selfies, can all magnify any insecurity you might have, especially when you are exposed to so many 'perfect'-looking images online.

Whatever makes you feel your body isn't 'right', weight-loss adverts and accounts on social media might look like the place to find help. But they aren't. There are many forums about diets and restrictive eating that lead to a rabbit hole of threads and groups encouraging or glamorizing **eating disorders,** such as **bulimia** and **anorexia,** as well as **self-harm.** Before you know it, you could find yourself in **a very dark place.**

Wanting to feel more in control, and developing obsessive behaviour over an aspect of your life, such as eating, is a sign of **STRESS.**

It's a sign that you need to **take care of YOURSELF,** rather than take your feelings out on your body. It's also a sign that you need to ask for help.

See **Chapter 17** for more about this.

In pursuit of perfection

Adverts for 'bum-lifting' jeans and 'sculpted abs' workouts might seem harmless, but the advertising industry's <u>focus on a certain body type, and persistent altering of images</u> to match it, can have a **BIG IMPACT** on the way we view ourselves and others.

It can lead to:

BODY-SHAMING of anyone who doesn't look like the photos, perhaps through public trolling or direct message bullying.

BODY DYSMORPHIA, where someone becomes obsessed over a perceived flaw in their appearance that their mind has invented or exaggerated.

Obsessive exercising and disordered eating as a result of BODY ANXIETY.

Increasing numbers of COSMETIC SURGERIES – extreme and very expensive steps to take to achieve a particular face or body type.

Don't put too much value on the number of likes and followers of accounts promoting physical 'ideals'. They are intended to attract lots of people, to boost sales. Searching for positive feedback on your photos and measuring your self-worth against others in likes and followers **won't ever make you feel as good about yourself as SELF-ACCEPTANCE will.**

Airbrushed and repetitive beauty images **DON'T** reflect most of the people you'd pass by in the street. They're **NOT** designed for you to relate to, but to **ENVY**. So <u>it's important not to be fooled into thinking these images are the real-life norm</u>, or 'standard'. Instead of being disappointed if real life doesn't match up to the photos, we should be disappointed about how these fake photos came to have such power over our health and happiness.

Self-esteem and what to do about it

There are some things you can do to improve your self-esteem and body image, and even contribute to helping others feel better about themselves...

☑ You could choose **NOT TO USE FILTERS** on your own photos, and **EMBRACE YOUR NATURAL SELF**; show life as it really is. The more people who do this, the more diverse the pool of images on social media will become.

☑ Actively **CELEBRATE DIFFERENCE**, individuality and uniqueness in your photos.

☑ Be brave and others will follow you. **USE POSITIVE WORDS** when you describe yourself, or just **DON'T TALK NEGATIVELY**. Even if you feel rubbish that day, you don't need to join in if other people are complaining about themselves. Instead, if you say something positive about others, they will likely say something positive about you, and everyone will feel happier.

☑ Stop following social media accounts that promote changes you should make to the way you look, and instead **FOLLOW ACCOUNTS THAT PROMOTE DIVERSE BODY TYPES.**

Ultimately, **give yourself a break.** Don't get hung up on airbrushed images of 'dream' bodies... just scroll on past. Appreciate all the limbs and senses and physical abilities you have – be grateful for them.

If you are kinder to yourself, you'll be able to be kinder to and **less judgemental** of others. And, in turn, if you are less critical of others, it will help you to be less critical of yourself.

Thanks, feet. You did a good job today.

Chapter 13

Strangers and direct messaging

Whether you are using a public-facing social media app, or a more friends-focused one, most apps will include a facility that allows you to send someone a **direct message** (a 'DM') that only they can see, which is useful when you want to have a private conversation with someone in the app.

...but, BEWARE!

Even if your messages are not public, that **DOESN'T** mean you can write mean or inappropriate things to someone else and get away with it – harassment or bullying via direct messaging can still be reported through the app.

Direct messaging with new people you've only spoken to on social media may not always be a good idea. It's best to **keep some distance and chat in the open** until you learn more about them and what they might be looking for in a new online friend.

Making new friends

Social media is a great place to find like-minded people, perhaps through a forum about your favourite TV show, or a group that plays your favourite sport. You might meet new friends on a gaming platform or fan site.

If you get to know someone whilst chatting on the main app, BEFORE you direct message, you'll be able to get an idea of whether they are someone you want to have a one-to-one conversation with. You don't necessarily want to be bombarded with messages from a super-chatty stranger.

Hello

Hi

Are you awake?

Hello

Hi

Hello

43 MESSAGES WAITING

Hey

Hey

Hi

197

Someone who is not your friend or contact could easily direct message you on social media unless your <u>privacy settings are **HIGH**</u>. It's a good idea to double-check your privacy settings every now and then, so you don't get unwanted messages from strangers.

Some apps have features that allow you to

DISABLE DIRECT MESSAGES

from anyone who isn't one of your contacts, so it's worth looking at what options are available to you in the settings part of the app.

In the shadows

Some groups prefer to hide behind all the chatter and activity on social media to avoid easy detection and make their club more exclusive – perhaps allowing people to join on recommendation only, or after an interview. This might sound tempting, **BUT these groups stay under the radar for a reason.** Some organizations that are <u>banned</u> in various countries try to use social media as a place to mobilize and attract new followers and members.

When an organization, club or group is 'banned', it means being a member of that organization is ILLEGAL. This is usually because the organization is based on EXTREMIST IDEOLOGY, which means members have strong views that some people should not be able to have their own rights, faiths and beliefs. They are also referred to as 'hate groups' because they promote hostility and even violence towards certain people, based on gender, race, religion, sexuality, disability and so on. Those that are banned are usually believed to organize acts of TERRORISM.

Radicalization

Members of extremist groups use social media, including gaming sites, to recruit people to join them. They may do this through videos, images and posts encouraging hate or glorifying violence. The articles and images they promote are **biased,** which means they are one-sided, and often misleadingly created by them in order to support their view, which is called **propaganda.**

Extremists use powerful language and are very passionate about their cause – they are keen to connect with young people who may be questioning some aspect of their lives, such as their relationship with their friends or parents, their status and belonging in school, their faith or identity. When extremists successfully convince someone to share their views, that person is said to have become **radicalized**.

How does it happen?

Radicalization is easiest to do **out of the public eye,** so extremists will try to start a conversation via direct message. Conversations start off general and friendly, but become more intense over a period of time until the extremist demands something and may make threats.

Let's talk in private...

If you do start a direct message conversation with a stranger, <u>look for these signs</u> to help you spot any **attempts at radicalization...**

WATCH OUT
for someone who...

⚠️ Flatters you or really sucks up to you.

⚠️ Tries to make you feel special to gain your trust.

⚠️ Tells you not to mention a conversation to anyone else, or asks you to keep secrets.

⚠️ Tells you that you can't trust your friends and family.

⚠️ Suggests they are here for you, but certain people in society are against you.

⚠️ Likes to talk in depth about 'right' and 'wrong', and has strong views on this.

⚠️ Suggests they can help give your life meaning.

Tell a trusted adult if __ANYONE__ you talk to online does __ANY__ of these things.

If you don't have an adult you feel comfortable talking to, you can find links to helplines and websites at **Usborne Quicklinks** (see page 4).

It's easy to accept a contact or DM request without thinking – after all, you are using an app designed for being social. But if someone you don't know asks to direct message you, ask yourself:

"Why don't they want to chat in the open?"

They may have a **hidden agenda**, which are intentions that you won't become aware of until you are deep in conversation and it's more difficult to walk away.

IRL ('in real life')

When you meet people solely through social media, you won't always be able to tell if they are really who they say they are.

Remember:

ANYONE you don't know well or haven't met is a **STRANGER**.

I am always honest.

Pati_Cake_9

I'll say my name is Ben. (It's not.)

Ben_G_121

xX.Sur1_S

This profile photo isn't me.

Real_Carl05

You don't know my full name.

It might be tempting therefore to suggest, or agree to, meeting up in person to get to know each other better. But meeting a <u>stranger</u> in person, even in a public place, even with a friend, and even if someone knows where you are, isn't wise. The stranger might be a harmful adult and **not the person you expected**, and you can't guarantee they will even be alone.

IT COULD BE VERY UNSAFE.

Grooming

Unfortunately, some adults use social media with bad intentions. Some want to seek out young people to talk to them in a sexual way, which is known as (**grooming**).

These people are called 'sexual predators', and they often create a **fake social media persona, with fake photos,** to pretend to be a young person. Their aim is to connect with a young person on social media, then gain their trust and get close to them, in the hope of developing a sexual relationship.

'PRIYA', '15' ...BUT, ACTUALLY IS ALEX, 47

// MY NAME IS PRIYA. I'M 15. //

WATCH OUT
for someone who...

⚠️ Flatters you, praising your selfies and your appearance – they might be trying to make you feel special to gain your trust.

⚠️ Tells you not to mention a conversation to anyone else, or asks you to keep secrets.

⚠️ Tells dirty jokes, or changes the subject to something sexual.

⚠️ Asks you personal questions, especially about your body.

No one else will understand.

> **YesWay_Jose_T**
> I love pugs and I collect hats.

> **Di.Lara.xo**
> @YesWay_Jose_T OMG! Me too. Twinning!

⚠️ Mirrors all of your opinions and interests – predators often pretend to like the same things as you.

⚠️ Says they want to be your boyfriend or girlfriend, even though you've never met.

Tell a trusted adult if <u>ANYONE</u> you talk to online does <u>ANY</u> of these things.

GROOMING IS A CRIMINAL OFFENCE.

If you think someone is grooming you, <u>report them through the app</u>. Some apps and websites have a special button called 'CEOP' that you can click to report grooming to the UK National Crime Agency.

209

Inappropriate messages

If you direct message with someone you only know on social media, or even with an adult you know in real life, **you should be particularly <u>careful</u> about the messages you send them.** By using social media, an adult can talk to you while you're alone, without anyone else knowing.

Are you in your room?

Can we chat alone?

Even if messages from an adult you know seem harmless, **show them to a parent or carer.** It's best that they know if adults are trying to talk to you online, so they can help to **KEEP YOU <u>SAFE</u>.**

If you find yourself about to send any sexual messages or images, **STOP AND THINK** about whether you really trust this person with your <u>privacy</u> and your <u>online reputation</u>.

See **Chapter 14** for more about this.

// CAN YOU SEND ME A NICE PIC OF YOU? //

NEVER give strangers your <u>address, location or contact details</u>, and DON'T TELL THEM TOO MUCH about <u>yourself and your daily life</u>. If a harmful adult can build up a picture of you, including the area you live in and places you often visit, they could come to find you.

KTsKite

Hey, are you ok? Not heard from you for ages.

MissT.Surfer

Sorry, met a guy on social...! Got a bit wrapped up in messaging.

KTsKite

Ah ok. What's he like, tell me everything!

MissT.Surfer

He lives in France, he's got a motorbike(!!) He's SO funny.

KTsKite

Jealous! But are you sure he's legit?! I'd be wary if I were you...

MissT.Surfer

Mmm, he really likes me. But yeah, maybe he's a bit too perfect...

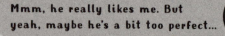

Chapter 14

Sexual content

Spend long enough on social media and you're likely to see something sexual - perhaps a photo, a video, or someone talking about

SEX.

Whether you feel ready for that or not, you need to know how to navigate social media <u>SAFELY</u> when it comes to sexual images, to **protect yourself** emotionally and legally.

Porn

There are images and videos of people having sex. This is called **pornography,** or **porn.** Whether you try to seek this out, or stumble across it online, there are laws in most countries stating the age you are allowed to view porn (for example, it is 18 in the UK).

While you're unlikely to be arrested for viewing porn, these age limits are there for a reason. Porn is created as a type of **entertainment.** <u>And, like in any film, or advert, it's all acting</u>. Watching it can give you unrealistic and damaging ideas about real-life sex and bodies, and might give you the impression that sex is about doing all kinds of things you might not be comfortable with.

I'm not sure I'm into that.

Every body is different

Porn stars may have fake breasts or shave off all their pubic hair. Seeing bodies like this can give people unrealistic expectations of what their, or someone else's, body should look like. There is no one way you should look. **Everyone is different in real life, which is GOOD!**

Some people can develop an unhealthy addiction to porn, and start to feel they **NEED** it every day.

For help with worries you may have about porn, see **Usborne Quicklinks** (page 4).

→ **YOU DON'T HAVE TO LIKE or** watch porn, or anything else, especially if it makes you feel uncomfortable.

→ **YOU DON'T HAVE TO LOOK at** anything sexual that your contacts are sharing on social media.

→ **YOUR FEELINGS MATTER and** if you don't want to look at a picture or video, that's totally up to you.

I want to be in control.

Don't be pushy

If you are in a relationship, you might feel you want to share pornographic images and videos with your boyfriend or girlfriend, **BUT don't just assume they will want to view these.**

They might not want to receive sexual comments from you on their social media, either, however flattering you think it is. And a stranger is unlikely to appreciate that kind of public attention from someone they don't know.

#cyber_flashing

Don't be tempted to direct message someone something sexual to flirt with them more privately. <u>They might take it a different way than you intended</u> and you could find yourself reported for harassment via the app. So, if in doubt, **DON'T SEND IT!**

Sexting

Sending 'nudes' (naked or partially-clothed photos) to someone is called (sexting). People who 'sext' usually send nude images of themselves, to someone they know or are in a relationship with.

Hey there...

!! CENSORED !!
!! CENSORED !!

If your boyfriend or girlfriend asks you to send intimate photos of yourself, or receive ones of them, you might not want to annoy them by saying no. **BUT** sending nudes to someone <u>if they, or you, are under 18</u> is **ILLEGAL** in many countries, including the UK.

If you share nudes with a boyfriend or girlfriend, you're unlikely to be prosecuted the first time, though the police may still want to investigate and check what's going on.

STOP! Questions to ask if you are being pressured into sending sexual content:

? Are you sending it because you really want to, or because other people do it?

? How would you feel if everyone in school saw this, or your parents, or strangers?

? What if this image or video remains online and is seen by a future employer?

? What would happen if you didn't send this – are you feeling threatened, or forced into it?

? Would you be willing to do this in real life? You might not feel ready, or be old enough, to start having sex, so are you really ready to send sexy pictures?

Once it's gone, it's gone

Even if you completely trust your boyfriend or girlfriend, it's still possible for pictures to <u>spread beyond</u> the person you sent them to. You're just a few slips of the thumb away from (**going viral**) without your underwear on.

If you have sent sexual content, that doesn't give someone the right to forward or show your messages to others. However, <u>you can't control what anyone else does with your messages and pictures</u> once you send them, so it's always better NOT to send something you might later regret.

Nooo! I've changed my mind!

Can I say no?

YES! Your body is **YOURS,** and what you do with it is up to **YOU** and no one else. If your boyfriend or girlfriend (or anyone else) asks you to send them a sexual photo or video of yourself - **stay safe, and say "NO"!**

Staying within the law

Even if you don't send nude photos to your boyfriend or girlfriend, they shouldn't send them to you, either. It is **ILLEGAL** to possess sexual images of someone under 18 (even if you are also under 18), which includes having those images or videos on your phone, laptop or in the cloud. The same goes for distributing (sharing) nudes of anyone under 18 (these images are classed as child abuse). So if you get sent nudes, DON'T forward them. **It's not just cruel; it's breaking the law.**

If someone sends you nudes of themselves, or someone else, or sends you <u>any kind of unwanted sexual content</u> on social media, you can **REPORT IT** in the app. Make sure you also tell a trusted adult, who could help you to report it to the police.

No, I don't want to see it from another angle, thanks.

NO.

One of the most important things you can learn about sex is that **it's always, always ok to say "no".** Don't let anyone else tell you that you 'should' feel ready for something that makes you feel <u>uncomfortable</u>. **IT'S ALWAYS YOUR CHOICE.**

Consenting to sexual activity

Most countries have an age at which you can legally consent (agree) to sex and sexual touching - in the UK the age of consent is 16. If you are **YOUNGER** than this and the person you are considering having a sexual relationship with is **OLDER,** then <u>even if you give consent</u>, **they could be prosecuted.**

You should **NEVER** feel under pressure to perform sexual acts, or exchange sexual content with someone, <u>whether you are in a relationship with them or not</u>. If someone is badgering, threatening or pressuring you into doing something you don't want to do, tell a trusted adult or call a helpline.*

*Find out how to do this at
Usborne Quicklinks, see page 4.

Revenge porn

Pictures and videos don't always get shared by accident, or even 'just for a joke'. When someone shares naked images of an ex-girlfriend or ex-boyfriend in order to embarrass them, it's known as `revenge porn`.

The law around sexting is there to PROTECT you - anyone requesting or sharing sexual images of children (usually anyone under the age of 18) may be guilty of possessing or distributing child abuse images.

That means posting sexual images of under 18s online is ILLEGAL, so if you are a victim of revenge porn, there are steps you can take...

ACTION PLAN
TO TAKE A STAND
AGAINST
REVENGE PORN

- **REPORT THE IMAGES** through the website or app they have appeared on, and **UNTAG YOURSELF** from them if you can. The app should remove any nude photos.

- **TALK TO AN ADULT YOU TRUST**, who can contact the person who posted the images and demand they are deleted.

- If the images are not removed and deleted, you could **CONTACT THE POLICE**.

See **Usborne Quicklinks** (page 4) for more information about where to find help.

You are NOT powerless

Having your private sexual content shared more widely could be very distressing and really get you down. The situation may feel hopeless and you may not want to tell anyone about it in case they see the images too.

What can I do now? I feel so alone.

You may feel like things have got out of control, but remember it's your body, your photos, and you can handle it. **Circulating nude images of someone without their consent is legally abuse** and THEY should be in the spotlight for it, <u>NOT **YOU**</u>. You shouldn't be made to feel ashamed by someone else's actions.

You need **help and support** from someone, ideally an adult at school, or a family member. It might be your worst nightmare telling your family that you shared intimate photos or videos, but being **honest and upfront** will help you to keep your head up high and ride it out. You're not the first or last person who has been through this – it can happen to ANYONE, even celebrities.

Bullying

It's not uncommon to be bullied about your sexual images or messages if they go public online, or are seen by others at school. Unfortunately, even if you don't engage in sexting, sexual content can be spread MALICIOUSLY in other ways:

Digitally **pasting someone else's head** on a nude photo.

Generating images from an 'undressing' app.

'Upskirting', which is where someone secretly takes a photo up someone's skirt.

These are ALL forms of **sexual bullying**.
(In the UK, 'upskirting' is a crime.)

Trolls who post unwanted or sexual comments on your video or photo should <u>should</u> <u>ALWAYS</u> be:

- IGNORED
- BLOCKED
- and REPORTED THOUGH THE APP.

<u>If someone is creating sexual images of you or a friend,</u> make sure you **speak up** and **REPORT THEM,** whether it's through the app or to an adult at school. What they are doing may be ILLEGAL, and a trusted adult can help you get the images taken down and deleted.

Dumping me was a bad idea...

Blackmail

Some bullies may encourage you to create and send them sexual images or videos of yourself, with the aim of **blackmailing** you. <u>Sometimes bullies can be really hard to spot</u> – your friend, your boyfriend or girlfriend, a family member or adult you know, or someone you have met online, may turn out to be a bully when it comes to sex.

Bribes and blackmail are a telltale sign. A bully may try to bribe you into sending sexual photos, by offering you something you'd really like in return, such as tickets to a concert you want to go to...

...But once they have your photos, they could then blackmail you, which means they could threaten to show the images to your family or friends, or post them publicly online, unless you do something sexual for them.

STAY OFF CAMERA!

If someone asks you to chat to them on a webcam, or video chat in private, say **"NO"**. A bully might try to trick you into doing something revealing or sexual on camera. If you livestream, **YOU DON'T KNOW WHO IS RECORDING IT,** and it could be a blackmailer. **WEBCAMS CAN BE HACKED,** so close your computer when you're not using it, or cover the webcam up with a sticker. Do this to your phone, too.

Other tricks

Some bullies may see innocent photos of you online and try to convince you that they are sexual – perhaps saying that you are embarrassing or 'easy' for posting something like that, and you deserve to be treated badly as a result. They may pretend that sexual images of you are already online, or exploit the competitive nature of young people posting selfies and ask you to send photos in order to be 'ranked' or 'voted on'.

What to do about it

Bullies are awful, and these kinds of particularly devious bullies who play mind games, bribe and blackmail are usually adults. They might think they have power over you because you're younger, but what they are doing is ILLEGAL (even if they never touch you), and you have the law on your side.

Sexual bullying is **ABUSE**[*], and if you suffer it (whether it's online or not), it's important to:

TELL SOMEONE

TALK ABOUT YOUR FEELINGS

GET HELP

Even if you haven't had any physical contact with the bully, <u>any form of abuse can have a very</u> **powerful and upsetting** impact on you.

Remember...

<u>None of this is **YOUR** fault</u>, and you are NOT the one to be punished for it.

[*] For more information about sexual abuse and where to go for help, go to **Usborne Quicklinks** (see page 4).

Make sure you:

X __DON'T REPLY__ to someone threatening or trying to bribe or blackmail you.

X __DON'T SEND__ MORE PHOTOS.

✓ __DO TELL__ SOMEONE this is happening.

It might feel unnatural ignoring someone who is trying to make contact with you, but that will **keep YOU in control**.

Although it will be uncomfortable, __KEEP a RECORD__ of any abusive or inappropriate messages or images.

Evidence like this will help the police to prove the bully has committed a crime, and to be able to punish them.

Chapter 15

Going viral

When content posted online is shared far and wide across social media, it's known as 'going viral'. Sometimes people post content with the intention or hope of it going viral, and sometimes content goes viral unintentionally or maliciously.

I think I've gone viral.

Spreading the word

Content can spread quickly as lots of people share it with their contacts, and those contacts share it on to **THEIR** contacts, and so on. Content could end up being shared many times because it's **topical**, perhaps related to **something in the news,** or it might be something that lots of people find **funny** or **relatable.**

There are also situations where you might deliberately post something on social media in the hope that it will go viral because you want to **find, promote,** or **raise awareness of something.**

Examples include:

- Promoting an EVENT you are involved in.
- Raising the alarm — HIGHLIGHTING A SCAM that is doing the rounds.
- Raising the profile of a CHARITY or a particular campaign.
- Promoting SOCIAL CONNECTION — perhaps getting lots of people to send a lonely person birthday messages.

1,397

CONGRATS AHMET

 Ahmet, have a great day

Hey Ahmet! Happy Birthday :)

- Looking for **SPONSORSHIP** for a charity challenge.
- Trying to track down and **FIND** a missing person, object or pet.
- Trying to **REUNITE** people with a lost object, or thank them for something.

40 mins ago LA_amaZane

66 Found a book inscribed 'TO MY PIPPIKIN'. Help me find Pippikin! **99**

#hashtags

As well as having lots of shares, content can also spread by the use of hashtags. The **#** 'hash' symbol is known on social media as a hashtag. In most social media apps, when the hash symbol is put at the start of a word, the word is then 'tagged'. Hence the term 'hashtag'.

#everydayisaschoolday

Hashtags are a way of **organizing and grouping things** on social media so that you can <u>easily find</u> what you're interested in. When you click on a hashtag, you can see all the related content that has been tagged in the same way. A hashtag also acts like a (**keyword**) when you're searching for something online, bringing up lots of relevant results to help you find what you're looking for.

How to use hashtags

It has to be one word, so if you want to make a phrase a hashtag, you have to run all the words together: `#MaxZoomMusicRocks`.

Don't make the hashtag too long or it will be difficult to read!

`#watchingthenewshowwithkodypacyandsallyanndempseyonchann`

Hashtags should be used to highlight keywords and topics; it's pointless to hashtag random words such as `#amazing` `#feelings`.

Don't hashtag really common words or massive topics, such as `#love` or `#cars`. Hashtags should be specific, to help you and others filter out unrelated content.

Don't use loads of hashtags in your post, or your message will get confusing so people might just ignore it.

On-trend

The more people who use and share a particular hashtag, the higher profile the tagged content will become. When online content becomes REALLY popular and widely discussed on social media, it is said to be (**trending**).

Companies and brands like to have a social media 'presence'. Marketing departments come up with advertising **slogans** that they put a hashtag in front of, in the hope that the slogan will begin to trend on social media.

"Rise and Shine"
with
PowerBits
#wideAWAKEY

PING! PING! PING!

> Morning all. R U #wideAWAKEY
>
> very much NOT #wideAWAKEY
>
> YES! Been for a long run. I'm #wideAWAKEY
>
> Sun's up. I'm #wideAWAKEY

Anyone can create a hashtag with a word or phrase, but the more **specific** and **memorable** ones have more chance of standing out and going viral.

As well as in product and company marketing, hashtags are also used for **public health campaigns** and **government initiatives,** to make sure a message reaches <u>as many people as possible.</u>

#happyenvironmentday

#oneplanet

#ecofriendly

#socialchangeforall

#equality

#seatbeltssavelives

#diversability

People power

Social media is a unique platform for sharing something around the world VERY QUICKLY. Trending content - which can be started by anyone - can come to the attention of presidents, prime ministers, A-list celebrities, royal families and other powerful and influential people. The ability to <u>send a hashtag viral</u> on social media allows people with similar opinions to **join together, be heard, and to make a difference** by raising wider awareness of an issue.

Many high-profile campaigns and movements start out on social media. They could start from a **PETITION** that attracts a huge number of signatures, or a **POST FROM A CELEBRITY** that attracts a wave of support, or possibly a **GLOBAL NEWS STORY** that prompts a united reaction.

These movements and campaigns aren't just collective complaints, they promote **ACTIVISM**, suggesting actions and goals that will effect positive change in society. Activism can be about anything that <u>strikes a chord with a lot of people</u>, from campaigns to end poverty or racism, to movements promoting gender equality, and organized protests against political policies and climate change. You're never too young to be an activist.

#WoW Women of Wonder

We are all wonderful!

#WoW

#WoW

#WoW

Bad news

No one has **control** over how trending content spreads, which makes it <u>very hard to contain</u>. That can be a good thing for people who feel marginalized and want their voices heard, but it also means nasty things can reach lots of people, too.

Some **downsides of going viral** include:

👎 You could find an innocent photo of yourself that you posted online has jokey text added by someone else and becomes a viral meme, and your image becomes famous on social media without your consent.

👎 Discriminatory and even extremist content can receive so many comments, likes and shares that it starts to trend and appear everywhere you look on social media, which can be very upsetting, especially if it affects you personally.

Viral 'chain letters' are stories that promise a reward for you sharing them – such as a blessing, or a threat if you don't share them – such as a warning of bad luck. They are designed to play on your emotions, making you feel anxious, hopeful, or guilty, to convince you to pass the message on.

Amongst the ideas and opinions that spread virally, there can be **misinformation** and **propaganda**. It's not always easy to find the facts or work out what someone's agenda might be online. Read the next chapter to get some tips for separating FACT from FICTION on social media.

You shouldn't feel pressured or conned into sharing anything online. Share something ONLY because YOU TRULY WANT TO.

Al3x-the-great3st

Can you send this pic round of my dog Ruby? She's gone missing :'(

MissT.Surfer

Aw no! Yeah sure, have you posted it on social?

Al3x-the-great3st

Yup, #FindRuby, and there's more photos on there. She's not chipped.

MissT.Surfer

Ah ok. I'll tag my neighbour, she's a vet. She can look out for her.

Al3x-the-great3st

Thanks. Our dog walker's forwarded it to his contacts. Fingers crossed.

MissT.Surfer

Worth posting on the Hopclere Community page, too.

Chapter 16

Fake news

As people spend more and more of their time on social media, it naturally becomes a place where articles, reviews and events are shared, and news spreads FAST.

We love you, Maximus!

Friends, contacts, followers, lend me your ears.

Sometimes information about current events is **generated specifically to be circulated on social media.** These kinds of articles and posts are created for lots of different reasons, but if news <u>hasn't been reported or verified by mainstream news channels</u> it's likely to be made up – it's (**fake news**).

For this reason, it's important to be able to **examine information that comes from social media carefully,** to make sure you can <u>TRUST</u> it.

The hive mind

Social media is sometimes referred to as a **hive mind,** or a 'collective intelligence' because every second it receives thousands of contributions from its users – thoughts, opinions, facts, lies, creative content – all being shared between contacts **like one giant global brain.** When content begins to trend, it is as if the whole network of social media is coming together as one to focus on and promote that content.

That can be a <u>good thing</u> <u>OR</u> <u>a bad thing</u>, depending on what it is that social media is championing at any given time. You might think that thousands of brains are better than one, and if they agree on something, then that can be taken to be general knowledge. But that isn't the case if social media users are duped into accepting as knowledge, something that **isn't actually a fact.**

Bad science

Due to the ability of social media to amplify certain content, **misinformation** (unintentionally misleading information) posted with good intentions can end up **confusing and endangering** lots of people. Especially when outdated or disputed scientific articles are forwarded without being fact-checked.

WAA! They're coming!

PING!

There is often health misinformation around diet, vaccines and treatments for diseases such as cancer, but **misinformation can spread about ANYTHING.** All it takes is one person's post misinterpreting something, then it being seen by someone who feels it's worrying or important enough to share... and before you know it <u>something completely wrong is on its way to becoming accepted FACT</u> on social media, especially if someone with a high profile and lots of followers gets involved in the chain along the way.

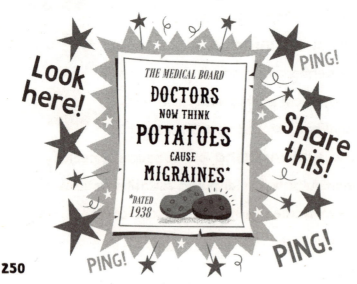

Look here!

PING!

THE MEDICAL BOARD
DOCTORS NOW THINK POTATOES CAUSE MIGRAINES*
*DATED 1938

Share this!

PING!

PING!

Disinformation

Some individuals and organizations use social media to spread **disinformation**, which is **biased or inaccurate content.** Usually they do it because they **hold genuine beliefs that they hope to convince others to share,** but, consciously or not, they selectively post information that seems to support their argument, and <u>IGNORE verified scientific findings</u> that dispute their claims.

As a result, the content they post is **one-sided, misleading** and, at worst, **dishonest.** Some spreaders of disinformation actively try to bury facts and instead use persuasive or fear-inducing language and creative content to raise their profile. They may also try to discredit experts in order to gain more attention and appear more authoritative.

The **POWER** of propaganda

The power of the social media hive mind is something that many people would like to harness. Some people may have straightforward intentions - perhaps to **raise awareness** of a little-known charity, **drive up sales** of a product, or **promote engagement with a cause.** Unfortunately, there are plenty of people who would like to use this power to push propaganda, which is <u>targeted disinformation</u>, created to influence certain sections of society.

Propaganda can be subtle. It's used to stoke distrust and discord, often for political purposes, which can be very destabilizing. An unstable and divided society is more vulnerable to attempts by individuals and organizations to impose their own form of control.

You will obey me.

Propaganda used by religious extremists, political fringe groups, hate groups and radical environmentalists can involve violent and upsetting imagery. Political propaganda (which is particularly rife around election time) is known as 'spin'. It might take the form of a **smear campaign,** where a politician or public figure is falsely discredited, undermined or has their reputation tarnished, as well as adverts designed to pit one group in society against another.

Propaganda can look very convincing and it's always designed to provoke an EMOTIONAL reaction. People who feel angry, scared, offended or excited are more likely to share content without considering its logic, origin or possible agenda.

OMG! I have to share this right NOW!

Artificial intelligence

Some organizations can be very devious and employ (deepfakes) and (bots) in their drive to manipulate opinion on social media.

You might think videos are the most truthful form of news, yet deepfakes are convincing videos of well-known people that have been CAREFULLY EDITED to make them appear to say things they never said. They are made to either discredit that person or imply that the person supports the creator's cause.

A video might be a deepfake, if:

- The person's EYE MOVEMENTS look unnatural, or unusual for them.

- The EMOTION on their face doesn't quite seem to match what they are saying.

- Their SKIN COLOUR, CLOTHING or FEATURES look slightly blurry or inaccurate.

- The AUDIO is inconsistent.

If you can slow down or zoom in on a video, that will help you to **examine it more closely.** You could also search for the video online, to see if there is an original version.

Bots (short for 'robots') are automated computer programs. Some can imitate human conversation patterns - to provide online customer service, for example. These 'chat bots' can also be used in large numbers by propagandists to infiltrate forums and pretend to be real people, influencing conversations and steering them in a particular direction. Bots can also repeatedly post disinformation to accelerate the spread of fake news.

BLIP-BEEP

// READ THIS. READ THIS. //

A social media account could be a bot, if:

BEEP
BLIP

- The profile has **NO PICTURE**, a bio with **TYPOS** and **NO FOLLOWERS**.
- The account posts a lot all day and night – **BOTS NEVER GET TIRED**.
- The account is **REPETITIVE** and talks about the same thing over and over, like a robot...

Why do we fall for it?

There are a few reasons why it's so easy to share questionable content:

1. Conspiracy theories can appeal to people struggling to make sense of events or issues they feel they have no control over.

2. Propagandists try to make their content look as credible as possible, so may use accounts impersonating a trustworthy source, such as a local newspaper, which gives the content an authentic appearance.

3. Content being shared by a number of people gives it some validation, and we tend to act in accordance with the majority.

4. Often it's our friends and contacts who have posted it, rather than strangers, and we trust our friends and those in our social circle.

The echo chamber effect

Your social media can act like an 'echo chamber', where your friends' and contacts' posts **reflect back your own views,** like an echo in a confined space.

Your friends and contacts might have similar opinions to you, and share similar stories, news articles and information. This means the (**personalization algorithms**) behind social media apps – which decide what to show on your newsfeed based on what you say you are interested in, and click on – might create such a **narrow focus of content** that differing views are edited out, and your social media experience becomes <u>biased</u>.

In this way, your view of the world can be <u>highly influenced by those you connect with on social media</u>, and can strengthen your **acceptance of misinformation.**

Your own network is only **A DROP IN THE OCEAN** online, so don't let the echo chamber convince you that everyone on social media thinks like **YOU.**

DON'T TRUST THE ALGORITHM

Social media newsfeeds prioritize popular content, making it even more popular, to the point where fake news can sometimes overwhelm real news. This is how conspiracy theorists can imply that experts and authorities won't be able to 'suppress the truth', when really it's very difficult to suppress a **LIE** once it is trending.

Critical thinking

Gossip, scandal and anything **SHOCKING** attracts more attention than other news, and sometimes **a rumour feels just too interesting not to pass on.**

However, the impact and volume of fake news can be so great, it's <u>every social media user's responsibility to make sure they don't spread lies and nonsense.</u>

Before sharing or posting a news article, use this list to work out if it's **TRUE**... or **NOT**.

FACT OR FICTION?

- Don't share a story based on the headline, make sure you READ THE FULL ARTICLE and think about whether it's really credible.

- CHECK THE DATE of the publication to make sure it is current and up to date.

- Look up whoever authored this content to CHECK THEIR CREDENTIALS. Strange-looking URLs can give away that it is not a reputable news site.

- CHECK ELSEWHERE ONLINE to see if the story is backed up by mainstream news sites.

- CONSIDER THE LANGUAGE of the article. Legitimate journalism won't use slang or include sloppy grammar and punctuation, and is unlikely to be emotionally charged or inflammatory.

- Ask yourself "Why was this article written?" Does it seem to have a particular agenda, and is it one-sided? Try researching the other side of the argument to COME TO AN INFORMED OPINION.
- CHECK PHOTOS AND VIDEOS for signs of digital manipulation, such as blurriness and inconsistencies.

Propagandists like to plant seeds of doubt that can grow into great trees of distrust and fear, so **it's good to be a bit sceptical of any information presented as fact.** By critically evaluating online content you can learn to be more media-savvy, and ensure you're not fooled by fake news. The easiest rule to remember is:

Don't be ruled by
your emotions. THINK
before you like or share.

MinotaurQue5ta

Did you read about telegraph poles secretly having CCTV cameras?!

WrightRonWrites

Yeah I saw that, eye roll.

MinotaurQue5ta

But it makes sense! They're literally everywhere.

WrightRonWrites

Yeah, as are CCTV cameras... why in telegraph poles?!

MinotaurQue5ta

So the govt can spy on you **THROUGH YOUR WINDOWS.**

WrightRonWrites

Dude, they've totally got you. It's just stupid fake news.

Chapter 17

Protecting your mental health

It's important to look after your mental health when you use social media. As well as trying to keep up with all that's going on with your friends online, **there is a lot on there that you might NOT want to engage with but find hard to avoid,** such as trolls, sexual content, airbrushed images and fake scare stories. It can all make you feel a bit **negative** or **overwhelmed** sometimes, but there are plenty of steps you can take to look after your mental health, and to find help when you need it.

BRAIN

Are you ok?

There are many kinds of mental health
difficulties, some more severe than others.
They can all make life tough at times.
Three that often affect young people are:

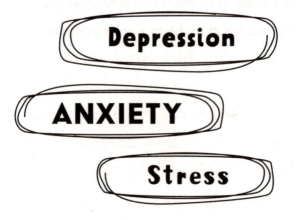

DEPRESSION is more than feeling a bit
fed up or pessimistic. People with depression
often have no energy or enthusiasm for things
they used to enjoy. They might not care about
their appearance or sleep well, and might
feel that they will never be happy again.

People suffering with **ANXIETY** feel worried, nervous, unsure, panicky or fearful – or all of these things at once – all, or a lot, of the time.

STRESS can stop you sleeping and make you feel on edge. It's natural to feel stressed sometimes, but it's a problem if your brain is in overdrive and you're feeling overwhelmed.

If any of these feelings seem familiar, it's worth taking a look at your social media use to see if it's making the problem worse, or if you could actually use it to help yourself FEEL BETTER.

I'm not sure I'm enjoying this much anymore.

Searching for help in the wrong place

It can be difficult trying to describe your emotions to others if you are feeling low, so some people take out their frustration on their bodies instead, by self-harming, restricting their eating, binge- or comfort-eating, or over-exercising. This may be because they can't find another way to express their pain, or unconsciously they want to feel in control of a significant part of their life.

If you feel compelled to do this then it's important to <u>ask for help</u>

– speak out, BEFORE you start to feel addicted to behaviour that could make you really unwell.

I need some help... I don't feel in control.

If you feel low, it might be tempting to search on social media for others who are also feeling this way. **BUT social media can be like a rabbit hole, and it's easy to get lost down it** once you start seeking out something negative. There are dark parts of social media – forums, websites, closed direct message groups – where people encourage punishing yourself, or others, in an effort to take away those bad feelings, when really that would make your situation even worse.

It's a better idea to seek help for your feelings **OFFLINE**, so you can talk to someone face-to-face or hear their voice. This can help to keep you grounded in reality, away from the screens, and give your tired mind a break.

I'd forgotten how nice it can be to see a friendly face.

Look away now

Even if you don't seek out upsetting things online, they may still pop up on social media because it's a space where lots of people feel comfortable chatting and sharing their thoughts and feelings. You might not feel

I know I'll feel bad if I look at that...

the same way, though, and **there might be things that you'd rather not talk about or see others mention.**

(Trigger warning) is a label someone can put at the top of their post to flag that it contains potentially upsetting content that might trigger (set off) a strong reaction in someone who identifies with it. They are often used by people who have recovered from something upsetting and now want to talk about it.

The important thing is to **acknowledge your own feelings,** and <u>DON'T view the content if you think it wouldn't be good for you.</u>

This show contains scenes that some viewers may find distressing.

<u>DO</u> use trigger warnings **YOURSELF** if you want to get something personal off your chest that might be difficult for others to read.

ALL my contacts will see this – and I don't want to upset anyone...

Don't buy into body negativity

There are, sadly, a lot of harmful adverts and promotions on social media that push the idea that there is something wrong with your body or face that needs fixing. Unsurprisingly, seeing these perceived criticisms alongside seemingly 'perfect' images can really dent your self-confidence.

When someone is trying to sell you something, <u>making you feel good **THE WAY YOU ARE** is **NOT** in their interests</u>. But **you can learn to build up a defence against the bombardment** of these images by spending a little bit of time each day practising good habits for a **POSITIVE** body image.

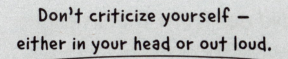

Don't criticize yourself — either in your head or out loud.

Instead, make positive statements, called
AFFIRMATIONS. It might feel embarrassing
to say these out loud at first, but if you keep
repeating them they can make a real difference.

Choose one of these statements
and say it RIGHT NOW...!

I am just as good as anyone else.

I respect my amazing body just as it is.

Nobody has the right to judge me on my appearance.

I am much more than how I look.

I am not an object to be looked at, I am a person looking out at the world.

I'm great!

Make sure your social media makes you feel GOOD - unfollow celebrity accounts that try to sell you products with their bodies, and instead <u>follow **BODY-POSITIVE** influencers.</u>

Move out from the limelight

It's easy to look at someone else's photos and posts on social media and THINK they are leading an amazing, charmed life. But projecting confidence and maintaining a shiny-looking profile can be <u>hard work</u>.

You can't edit real life, but you can spend a lot of time editing your online life to look as good as possible, **which can be a full-time job for celebrities and social media personalities.**

These people want their profile to attract attention, and to stand out from a very large online crowd. Others might edit their profiles in order to blend in with their friends.

The 'need to belong' is a powerful human urge, but so is the desire to be **special** and **unique.** Learning to balance those two things can be tricky on social media.

If you **have confidence in yourself,** that's half the battle. One way to protect your self-esteem and maintain confidence in yourself is to try not to let your sense of worth get tied up with the number of social media contacts and followers you have, or the number of likes and shares your posts get.

Chasing numbers like this is **STRESS you don't need.** However many followers you have, <u>all you need is one friend or family member to give you a hug when you need it</u>. Remember, a quick click on your post from a stranger – or not – isn't as important to your success in life as your own hard work and dedication.

Some social media apps allow you to **HIDE** the number of likes and other reactions your posts receive, which is useful if you're posting for meaningful engagement from your contacts, rather than sheer number of views.

Positive steps

None of us can control our lives as much as we might like, and **we certainly can't control other people and what they think of us.** By taking the weight of other people's opinions off your shoulders, you might find yourself feeling a lot better, mentally.

Try some of these ideas to **boost** and **protect** your mental health, including via social media.

KEEPING PERSPECTIVE

+ Try to be as hopeful and positive as you can, and see the good in people. Practising this will, over time, build your resilience, which helps you recover from setbacks or problems.

+ If you're overwhelmed, write out a list of your worries and try breaking down each problem into smaller steps. Dealing with them one at a time will help you work through it.

✚ If you feel anxious about a situation, look back at how you've responded to stressful things in the past. Was there something that worked that you could try again, or is there possibly a better way you could try this time? Learn from your mistakes, but also <u>recognize your successes</u>.

✚ Prioritize face-to-face time with your friends and family – don't say 'not now' – because when the going gets tough, they are the people you'll need to talk to. Having fun with your friends offline and <u>investing in your friendships</u> will reap rewards down the line.

A HEALTHY MIND AND BODY

✚ Make sure you <u>get enough sleep</u> – 8 to 10 hours a night. It's ESSENTIAL REST for your brain as well as your body. Sleep-deprivation can quickly lead to bad moods, headaches and restlessness.

✚ Eat well. <u>The food you eat really makes a difference to your mood</u>. Eating more colourful fruit and vegetables, instead of a lot of sugar and beige food, will help to keep you MORE alert and LESS prone to mood swings.

✚ Being online can make you feel stuck inside your own head. <u>You need to connect with your body too</u> — even if it's just dancing around your bedroom. Exercise releases chemicals in your body that make you feel good. If you find a physical activity that you enjoy and make time to do it regularly, you'll feel fitter, more energetic, and it will improve your mood and sleep.

✚ <u>Get outside. It's surprising how good fresh air and sunlight can make you feel.</u> Spending some quiet time in nature, even if it's just walking or sitting, helps to make you calmer, more clear-headed and able to put things in perspective.

✛ <u>Do something you LOVE, or
learn a new skill</u> — anything that
requires your focus or challenges
your brain for a while. Improving and seeing
results from your efforts really boosts your
self-confidence, and you never know where
a new skill or interest might take you in life.

✛ <u>Give up some time for others.</u> You could
volunteer for a charity, get involved in local
fundraising, or join a club to find a supportive
community. Even just growing and nurturing
a plant can give you a warm sense of pride.

POSITIVE SOCIAL MEDIA

✚ There are positive movements on social media that look to <u>support good mental health</u>. If you follow positive groups, sites and accounts, you may find some LITTLE RAYS OF HAPPINESS in your newsfeed, which can balance out the negative stuff that spreads much more easily.

✚ If you do see negative or inappropriate content, <u>report it yourself via the app</u> rather than wait for someone else to do it. This will benefit all users.

✚ When you come across something you think is uplifting — perhaps a quote, a real-life story or a supportive group — <u>share it with others.</u> And remember to BE KIND AND POLITE on social media, if you want the same in return.

Filtering out the noise

You don't have to scroll through photos and posts from people you'd avoid in the street.

On most apps you can **quietly unfollow, unfriend or otherwise disconnect from someone on your social media without them being notified about it.** You might be able to hide posts from certain people for a time, while you think about it.

The social media algorithm will select content from the contacts that you interact with the most on the app, so if you **keep your social circle small** on the app, that can help to keep your feed manageable and less overwhelming.

Taking a screen break

If you find being online is just making you more unhappy than not, **don't be afraid to STOP.**
You could choose to deactivate or suspend your social media account for a while (which is like hitting 'pause', without losing your profile or contacts), to give you some breathing space to work out what you want from social media and how to make it work better for you. You may even decide you want to go ahead and delete your account, perhaps to move to another app that you think is more suited to you, or for a permanent break.

CLOSED UNTIL FURTHER NOTICE

Let go of the 'FOMO' (Fear Of Missing Out) if you decide to step away from social media for a while. Instead, you can focus on creating real-world fun times and memories that others won't want to miss out on!

Social media glossary

app (application) – software designed
to run on a mobile device.

avatar – an illustrated figure representing
a person online, used instead of a photo.

bio (biography) – a short description about
someone, usually including their hobbies.

Bitcoin – a type of digital currency.

blog (weblog) – an informal and regularly
updated webpage written by a group or an
individual (called a blogger).

bot – a software program that runs
repetitive, automated tasks online.

browser history – a list of webpages a user has visited.

content – video, audio, text (such as messages and posts), photos or other images online.

content-creator – someone who regularly makes and posts **content** online for a particular purpose, such as entertainment, or education.

cookie – a small piece of **data** used to identify you as you browse a website.

crowdsourcing – a process to raise funds for a charity or project, from online supporters.

data – information produced or stored by a computer.

deepfake – audio or video of someone that has been digitally altered to appear to show someone else, or say something inauthentic.

digital footprint – traceable information left by someone following their online activity.

direct message – a private message between two users on a social media platform.

discussion thread – discussion of a particular topic on a **forum**, where all replies are grouped together.

emoji – small picture graphic, often of a facial expression, embedded in or added to text to convey an emotion.

fake news – false information broadcast or published as news, in order to deceive people.

feed (newsfeed) – a constantly updated webpage showing the latest posts and comments on a site.

filter – a way to edit photos and videos to create a particular feel or appearance.

follower (or **subscriber**) – someone who chooses to receive automatic updates from a particular social media account.

forum – a website or page where users post and reply to messages discussing a topic.

going viral – when **content** is shared rapidly across social media.

grooming – when someone builds up a trusting relationship with a young person, in order to manipulate or abuse them.

hacker – someone who uses a computer to gain unauthorized access to **data**.

hashtag – a word or phrase preceded by a **#** symbol, to identify **content** on a topic.

influencer – someone who is able to influence a large number of people on social media, by recommending products or services.

keyword – a search term on a website.

like – a signal of approval or agreement, via a clickable icon on a social media **app**.

link – highlighted text that sends the user to another online location when clicked on.

livestream – a live transmission of video or audio online.

malware (malicious software) – programs designed to disable, damage or steal **data**.

meme – a brief piece of **content**, created or adapted to be humorous, that **goes viral**.

network – a system of interconnected people.

notification – an alert from an **app** informing a user of new posts, messages or updates.

personalization algorithm – the part of an **app** that calculates what should appear on your **feed**, based on your personal **data**, **likes**, and websites you visit.

pop-up – an online ad that suddenly appears as a small window on your screen.

profile – a user's personal area or page on a social media **app** where they post **content**.

revenge porn – posting explicit images of someone online without their consent, in order to cause distress.

selfie – a photo you take of yourself, usually with a smartphone, to post on social media.

sexting – sending sexually explicit **content**.

share – forward, or re-post on social media.

subscriber (or **follower**) – someone who chooses to receive automatic updates from a particular social media account.

trending – currently popular or widely discussed **content**, especially on social media.

trigger warning – a statement at the start of a piece of **content** alerting viewers that it contains potentially distressing material.

trolling – posting something deliberately offensive or provocative to upset or anger other users.

URL (Uniform Resource Locator) – the address of a webpage.

vlog – a video **blog**. People who make vlogs are called vloggers.

website traffic – the volume of users visiting a website.

Index

A

B

C

Notes

Cover design by
Kirsty Tizzard

Additional design by
Ruth Russell

Proofreading by
Alice Beecham

Additional illustration by
Nancy Leschnikoff and Freya Harrison

Usborne Publishing Ltd., Usborne House,
83-85 Saffron Hill, London EC1N 8RT, England.
usborne.com
Printed in the UK. First published in 2022.
Copyright ©2022 Usborne Publishing Ltd. UKE.